Gospel in the Rosary

Bible Study on the Mysteries of Christ

Gospel in the Rosary

Bible Study on the Mysteries of Christ

By Daniel R. Sanchez, D.Min., D.Phil.

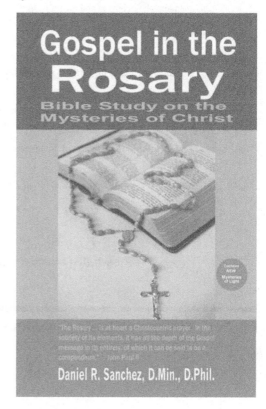

Gospel in the Rosary
Bible Study on the Mysteries of Christ

Requests for permission should be addressed in writing to: 3515 Sycamore School Road, Ft. Worth, Texas 76133 or contact us at the web site given below.

For more information about this book and other resources and training materials, or to contact the author, please refer to the Church Starting Network web site: www.churchstarting.net.

ChurchStarting.net Publications is an imprint of the Intercultural Institute for Contextual Ministry.

Church Starting Network is ministry of the Sanchez Center for Reproducing Congregations at the Intercultural Institute for Contextual Ministry.

Cover Photo:
Russell Illiq / Getty Images

Library of Congress Cataloging-in-Publication Data

Sanchez, Daniel R., 1936 —
Gospel in the rosary: Bible study on the mysteries of Christ. / Daniel R. Sanchez.
Includes bibliographical references.

ISBN # 1-894933-43-5

1. Rosary. 2. Meditations. 3. Rosary – meditations. I. Title.

BX2310. R7 S52
242.74

DEDICATION

We want to dedicate this book to every person in the world who has a soul thirst for a personal, spiritual relationship with Jesus Christ, the light of the world. "May Christ dwell in your hearts through faith, and may charity be the root and foundation of your life. Thus you will be able to grasp fully with the holy ones, the breadth and length and height and depth of Christ's love, and experience this love which surpasses all knowledge, so that you may attain to the fullness of God himself." (Ephesians 3:17-19).

ACKNOWLEDGEMENTS

We want to express our sincere gratitude to Jason S. Hiles for assisting us with the translation of portions of the manuscript for this book. We also want to thank Lou Ann Watke for her editorial work and Lisa Seeley and Georgette Lodwick for their assistance in the electronic formatting of the material for this book. Without their able and dedicated assistance, the publication of this book would not have been possible.

PREFACE

On the 16th of October 2002, Pope John Paul II sent an apostolic letter to the Bishops, Clergy, and faithful emphasizing the significance of the Rosary.[1] In this letter he affirmed the Rosary's "evangelical character and Christological inspiration."[2] He explained:

> In the sobriety of all of its elements, it has the depths of the Gospel message in its entirety, of which it can be said to be a compendium.[3] The Rosary, reclaimed in its full meaning, goes to the very heart of the Christian life; it offers a familiar yet faithful spiritual and educational opportunity for personal contemplation, the formation of the People of God, and the new evangelization.[4]

The Gospel of Jesus Christ is the means established by God for our salvation. St. Paul stated this fact correctly when he said: "I am not ashamed of the gospel. It is the power of God for the salvation of everyone who believes." By studying and meditating on the "Mysteries of Christ in the Rosary," we can come to a clearer understanding of the Gospel and come to know Jesus Christ as "Lord and Saviour."[5]

For centuries, the use of the Rosary has assisted many people in their prayer and devotional life. "The beginnings of the Rosary are found in the early Christian practice of reciting the 150 psalms from the Bible, either daily or weekly. Those unable to recite the psalms began to recite 150 prayers, mainly the Our Father, 150 times using beads to count their prayers." [6] The present form of the Rosary is believed to have originated through a coalescence of popular devotions from the 12th century onward. By 1573, an official feast was declared and the Rosary was made a part of the Roman Catholic Church's liturgical life.[7] Generally, the Rosary is begun with the Apostle's Creed, the Lord's Prayer, three Angelica Salutations, and one Glory Be to the Father.[8] When this is completed, people are encouraged to begin to meditate on the first mystery in the first series of mysteries.

Traditionally, these Mysteries included in the Rosary have been divided into three categories: *Joyful, Sorrowful,* and *Glorious.* The *Joyful Mysteries* described in the Bible include: The Annunciation of the Birth of Jesus to Mary; the Visitation of Mary to Elizabeth; the Nativity of Jesus; the

Presentation of Jesus in the Temple, and The Finding of Jesus in the Temple. The *Sorrowful Mysteries* in the Bible include: The Agony of Jesus in the Garden; The Scourging at the Pillar; The Crowning with Thorns; The Carrying of the Cross; and The Crucifixion and Death. The *Glorious Mysteries* in the Bible focus on: The Resurrection of Christ; The Ascension of Christ to Heaven; The Descent of the Holy Spirit at Pentecost; and The Return of Christ.[9]

In an effort to "bring out more fully the Christological depth of the Rosary,"[10] Pope John Paul II proposed the addition of five new "M*ysteria Lucis*" (Mysteries of Light or Luminous Mysteries), which focus on the three years of Jesus' public life, when he proclaims the Gospel of the Kingdom.[11] The *Luminous Mysteries* found in the Bible include: (1) The Baptism of Jesus in the Jordan; (2) his Self-manifestation at the Wedding of Cana; (3) his Proclamation of the Kingdom of God with his Call to Conversion; (4) his Transfiguration and; (5) his Institution of the Eucharist. Each of these mysteries is *a revelation of the Kingdom now present in the very person of Jesus.*[12]

These mysteries mentioned above form the core of the Gospel of Jesus Christ. The Apostle Paul gave a concise definition of the content of the Gospel he received from Christ: "that Christ died for our sins in accordance with the Scriptures, that he was buried; that he was raised on the third day in accordance with the Scriptures;" (1Corinthians 15:3-4). Christ's death, burial, and resurrection took place "in accordance with the Scriptures." This means that these events occurred according to the purpose and with the results described in The Holy Bible. Jesus died in our place, satisfying the demands of God's holiness. He rose bodily from the grave. Through personal faith in Him, we can be delivered from eternal punishment in hell and live eternally in His presence in heaven (Romans 10:8-13).

In his discourse at Pentecost (recorded in Acts chapter 2), St. Peter also presented a concise explanation of the Gospel when he spoke about the death of Jesus (v. 23), the resurrection of Jesus (vv.24-32), the ascension of Jesus (v.33-36), the coming of the Holy Spirit (v.33; 38; 39), and the salvation that people can receive by repenting of their sins and placing their trust in Jesus as their savior (v.38).

The Gospel, therefore, is the Good News that Jesus was born of the Virgin Mary, died on the cross for our sins, rose from the dead, went up to heaven, and sent his Holy Spirit to live in our hearts. If we place our trust in Jesus, we will be forgiven of all of our sins, experience his presence in our daily lives, and go to heaven with him when we die (John 14:1-3).

In this book we focus on the *Joyful, Luminous, Sorrowful,* and *Glorious Mysteries* that relate closely to the life of Jesus and that are clearly presented in the Bible. In keeping with the affirmation of John Paul II "that everything in the life of Jesus is a sign of his Mystery"[13]and that there is a need to supply the Biblical foundations on which the mysteries are based,[14]additional Bible studies have been included under the *Glorious Mysteries.* These focus on two dialogues that Jesus had (Nicodemus, the Samaritan Woman) and two parables that he taught (the Prodigal Son, the Rich Man and Lazarus). Through these Bible lessons we can come to a clearer understanding of the love of God and of the mission of Jesus to draw us near to our Heavenly Father, and to prepare us for our life with him in heaven.

People are encouraged to meditate on the Mysteries of Christ in the Rosary. In each of these Bible studies, therefore, there will be opportunities to meditate on the significance of the lessons of these Mysteries for our relationship with Jesus Christ. John Paul II said, "In order to supply a Biblical foundation and greater depth to our meditation, it is helpful to follow the announcement of the mystery with the proclamation of a related Biblical passage, long or short depending upon the circumstances. No other words can match the efficacy of the inspired word. As we listen, we are certain that this is the word of God, spoken for today and for me."[15] He also suggested: "Without in any way diminishing the value of such invocations, it is worthwhile to note that the contemplation of the mysteries could better express their full spiritual fruitfulness if an effort were made to conclude each mystery with *a prayer for the fruits specific to that particular mystery.*"[16] In keeping with these valuable suggestions, at the end of each mystery, we have included a Bible verse to be memorized and a prayer for the fruits of that mystery. May the blessings of God be upon you as you diligently study and meditate upon his Holy Word.

END NOTES

[1]   John Paul II. *Apostolic Letter Rosarium Virginis Mariae of the Supreme Pontiff* http://www.vatican.va/holy_father/john_paul_ii/apost_letters/documents/hf_jp-ii_apl_20021016_rosarium-virginis-mariae_en.html

[2]   Ibid., 2.

[3]   Ibid., 1.

[4]   Ibid., 2.

[5]   Ibid, 1.

[6] Rev. Victor Hoagland, C.P., The Scriptural Rosary, (New York: The Regina Press, 1999), 7.

[7] Reynolds R. Ekstrom and Rosemary Ekstrin, Concise Catholic Dictionary, (Mystic, Ct: Twenty-Third Publications, 1991), 131.

[8] Felician A. Foy, editor, Catholic Almanac, (Huntington: Our Sunday Visitor, Inc, 1992), 325.

[9] This Mystery is not included in the traditional Rosaries. In keeping with John Paul II's assertion that Luminous Mysteries draw the mind to a more expansive reflection of the rest of the Gospel, we have included the Mystery of Christ's return. See John Paul II, Apostolic Letter, 15,16.

[10] John Paul II, Apostolic Letter, 9.

[11] John Paul II, Apostolic Letter, 11.

[12] John Paul II, Apostolic Letter, 11.

[13] John Paul II, Apostolic Letter, 13.

[14] John Paul II, Apostolic Letter, 22.

[15] John Paul II, Apostolic Letter, 16.

[16] John Paul II, Apostolic Letter, 18.

Table Of Contents

PART TWO: The Luminous Mysteries

PART THREE: The Sorrowful Mysteries

PART FOUR: The Glorious Mysteries

PART ONE:

THE JOYFUL MYSTERIES

The *Joyful Mysteries* describe the happiness that the coming of Jesus brought to the lives of people. At the Annunciation the angel Gabriel said to the Virgin Mary: "Hail, Favored one!" (Luke 1:28) When the Virgin Mary went to visit Elizabeth the presence of Christ in her womb caused John to "leap for joy" (cf. Luke 1:41). When Jesus was born, the angel said to the shepherds: "Do not be afraid; for behold, I proclaim to you good news of great joy that will be for all the people. For today in the city of David a savior has been born for you who is Messiah and Lord" (2:10, 11). At the Presentation of Jesus in the Temple, Simeon with great joy took Jesus in his arms and blessed him in these words: "Now, Master, you may let your servant go in peace, according to your word, for my eyes have seen your salvation, which you prepared in sight of all the peoples, a light for revelation to the Gentiles, and glory for your people Israel" (Luke 2:29-32). There was joy in the hearts of Mary and Joseph when they found the twelve-year-old Jesus in the Temple. In sorrow they had searched for him, but they experienced joy when they found him "sitting in the midst of the teachers, listening to them and asking them questions" (Luke 2:46-49). As we study the passages and meditate upon the lessons of the *Joyful Mysteries,* may we experience the joy of coming to know Jesus as our personal Savior.

THE ANNUNCIATION OF THE BIRTH OF JESUS
(Luke 1:26-38)

One of the happiest moments in the life of a couple is when they receive the news that they are going to give birth to their first child. When my wife and I listened to the doctor telling us that we were going to have a child, we felt a special emotion thinking that we were participating with God in the miracle of the creation of a human being. Our lives were going to have a different significance. Now we could not live only for ourselves, but rather live to love, to nurture, to protect, and to guide the baby that would be born as a result of our love. Immediately we began to imagine what our child would be like and what he or she would become in life. Our happiness became even greater when we began to share the good news with our parents, with other acquaintances, and with our close friends. These were beautiful moments. Not only did we feel happy about the news that we had received, but we also felt surrounded by people who loved us and who were there to help us prepare ourselves for this new experience in our lives.

In one way the announcement of the birth of our child was similar to the announcement of the birth of Jesus. It was a new experience; there was much happiness and anticipation of the arrival of the child, and many other people rejoicing in the news. But, in another way, the announcement of the birth of Jesus was totally different from the announcement that we received about the birth of our child.

The Meaning of the Annunciation

The annunciation of the birth of Jesus was unique for many important reasons. This announcement was given supernaturally. It was not a doctor but rather an angel who made the announcement. The announcement did not refer to an ordinary person, but rather to an extraordinary person who would be different from all of the human beings that had existed since the creation of the world. His conception would not be the product of the union of a man and his wife but rather a miraculous conception. His origin would not be earthly but divine. His mission would not be simply to reach personal goals but rather the salvation of humanity. His reign would not be earthly and temporal but spiritual and eternal. This was the annunciation of the birth of the Son of God. For that reason the annunciation was more important and more glorious than any other announcement that would ever be made. Although it was made 2000 years ago, this announcement has great significance for our lives today and for our eternal destiny. Let's study the significance of this marvelous announcement. In the first chapter of the gospel according to Luke, we find the description of this announcement.

An Announcement of the Supernatural Birth of Jesus

The announcement of the birth of our Lord Jesus Christ was supernatural for various reasons. In the first place, it was given by an angel. The 26th verse says: "In the sixth month, the angel Gabriel was sent from God to a town of Galilee called Nazareth."

The expression "in the sixth month" refers to the pregnancy of Elisabeth, the mother of John the Baptist. In verses 5 through 25 of the same chapter we read that Elisabeth and Zechariah, who was a Jewish priest, were advanced in years and did not have children. One day, while Zechariah was fulfilling his duties as priest in the sanctuary, the angel Gabriel appeared to him and gave him the news that Elisabeth was going to have a son (vv. 11-13). Because this seemed impossible to him, due to the advanced age of himself as well as his spouse, Zechariah asked the angel to give him a sign that this was a real appearance and that the angel had really been sent by God (v. 18). So that Zechariah would believe, the angel identified himself and told him "I am Gabriel" (the name means *the mighty one of God*). Next the angel told him that because he had not believed the message, Zechariah would be left mute until the birth of the child (v. 20). In verses 57-66 we find the description of the birth of John the Baptist. But before that birth, Gabriel was sent to make the announcement of a more important birth. And so, it was in the sixth month of the pregnancy of Elisabeth that the angel Gabriel appeared to give the announcement of the birth of Jesus. It was a supernatural announcement because it was made by an angel.

In the second place, this announcement was supernatural because it was given to a virgin. The 27th verse says: "to a virgin betrothed to man named Joseph, of the house of David, and the virgin's name was Mary." To understand the expression "a virgin betrothed," we have to know something about the Jewish customs regarding marriage. One year before the wedding, one had a ceremony that was similar to what we know as the giving of an engagement ring. In this ceremony the couple announces that they have plans to be married. This ceremony is different from an engagement ring ceremony in that the chosen bride already belonged to the husband and nothing could end the wedding plans except for divorce or death. Although they were not permitted to have sexual relations until after the wedding, being pledged meant that they belonged to one another. It is important to note that the announcement of the birth of Jesus was made to a lady that was pledged but was not married. After more consideration, we can see how the idea, that Jesus was born of a virgin guarantees that his birth has to be a miracle of God. The fact that the announcement was made was by an angel to the virgin makes this announcement truly supernatural.

An Announcement of the Divine Origin of Jesus

Not only the announcement but also the origin of Jesus was supernatural. The angel told Mary "you will conceive in your womb and bear a son, and you shall name him Jesus" (v. 31). Listening to these words Mary was filled with joy. It was surprise enough seeing an angel (v. 28), but listening to the announcement that she was going to have a son seemed impossible. Then she asked him: "How can this be, since I have no relations with a man?" (v. 34). In certain cases in the Bible the word *relations* is used to refer to marriage union (see Genesis 4:1). Mary was saying, how can I have a son considering that I have not had sexual relations? "The angel said to her in reply, The Holy Spirit will come upon you, and the power of the Most high will overshadow you" (v. 35). The angel was telling her was that this birth was going to be different from all other human births. This birth was not going to involve a man. The cell of life was not going to come from a man but rather God himself. The Holy Spirit of God was going to work a miracle and was going to form that cell of life in Mary's womb. This is what would make the virgin birth of a child possible. For that reason our Lord Jesus Christ is different from all of humanity. He was born of a virgin.

But there is another thing that makes Jesus' life different. He is the Son of God. The 32nd verse says: "He will be great and will be called Son of the Most High." The 35th verse adds: "Therefore the child to be born will be called holy, the Son of God." This is the miracle of miracles. This Son of God came from heaven to earth to be born of a virgin. The gospel according to John explains this when it says: "And the Word became flesh and made his dwelling among us, and we saw his glory, the glory as of the Father's only Son, full of grace and truth." (John 1:14). Jesus, then, is the Son of God that came to earth, taking human form to share with us the love of God. As a human, born of the womb of Mary, Jesus can understand our struggles, our suffering, our fears, and our weaknesses. As God, the Son of the Most High, he can forgive our sins, change our lives, give us hope for the future, bring peace to our hearts, and grant to us the power to overcome temptations.

CHAPTER 1

An Announcement of the Saving Mission of Jesus

In addition to telling Mary that she would be an instrument in the hands of God for the birth of his son, the angel explains what will be the mission of Jesus. Luke 1:31 says: "and you shall name him Jesus." In the Jewish culture the name Jesus is a form of the name Joshua, which means "salvation of Jehovah." The gospel according to Matthew explains this when it says, "She will bear a son and you are to name him Jesus, because he will save his people from their sins," (Matthew 1:21). This makes it clear that the mission of Jesus is to save us from our sins.

Zechariah, the father of John the Baptist, also spoke about the mission of Jesus. After the birth of his son, Zechariah gave God's message that explained what would happen to Jesus, our Lord.

First, Zechariah said that John the Baptist came "to give his people the knowledge of salvation through the forgiveness of their sins," (Luke 1:77). John the Baptist introduced Jesus, the one who would forgive our sins. The people of Israel had separated themselves from the commands of God. They had come to a place in which they practiced religion in a legalistic and superficial way. They were simply following the rites and the ceremonies of the Jewish religion, but not having true devotion and not living lives that pleased God. For that reason God, through his prophets, had said to them: "This people honor me with their lips, but their hearts are far from me" (Matthew 15:8). It was necessary for Jesus to come so that the people could receive the salvation of God. This salvation includes the "forgiveness of sin." This forgiveness means that people now do not have the burden of guilt in their hearts. It also means reconciliation with God. Now they can feel close to God, accepted by Him and converted into recipients of his love.

Second, the "knowledge of salvation" came "because of the tender mercy of our God, by which the rising sun will come to us from heaven." Jesus came not because human beings were pleasing to God with their lives and their religious practices, but rather because God is filled with mercy. Jesus likewise explained this when he said, "For God so loved the world that he gave his only Son, so that everyone who believes in him might not perish but might have eternal life" (John 3:16). It was this mercy that made God send his Son to this world.

Third, Jesus came "to shine on those who sit in darkness and death's shadow" (v. 79). Before the coming of Jesus, the people walked in the darkness of sin and in superstition and ignorance. This spiritual darkness caused people to live in "death's shadow." Now knowing the truth of God, continuing in their darkness and in their sin, they came close to spiritual death, the complete separation from God.

Fourth, Jesus came "to guide our feet into the path of peace" (v. 79). When he gave them this message, there was much conflict between the Jewish people and the Roman government. In addition to this, there was great conflict in the hearts of the people because they did not know how to deal with their feelings of guilt and spiritual void in their lives. The apostle Paul speaks about this peace that Jesus came to bring when he says, "since we have been justified by faith, we have peace with God through our Lord Jesus Christ" (Romans 5:1). When we put our faith in Jesus Christ as our Savior, we are justified, and placed in a correct relationship with God, and this produces a deep peace in our hearts.

There are many sincere and religious people who do not know why Jesus came to this world. Some of them believe that Jesus came to teach us how to die. Although it is true that Jesus died an exemplary death, he did not come to teach us how to die, but rather to teach us how to live. Jesus said, "I came so that they might have life and have it more abundantly" John 10:10). This abundant life includes what Zechariah said about the mission of Jesus. Let us take a few moments to think about the significance of this for our life.

1. What is significant to us about the fact that Jesus came to forgive our sins?

2. What does it mean that Jesus came to share with us the love of God?

3. What does it mean that Jesus came to take us out of our darkness and give us the knowledge of the truth of God?

4. What does it mean that Jesus came to bring peace to our hearts?

5. Thinking of the significance of the mission of Jesus the Lord of our lives, another question emerges: How should I respond to this demonstration of love on the part of God?

The Response of the Virgin Mary to the Announcement

The way in which the Virgin Mary responded to the message of the angel is an inspiring example for us.

Mary Showed an Open Mind

Luke 1:28 says that the angel went to her and said, "Hail, favored one! The Lord is with you." The root of the word *favored* is the word *grace*, which means "unmerited favor with God." The reason that she was favored and blessed is found in the expression "the Lord is with you." This grace and this blessing come from God himself.

The appearance of the angel as well as his words surprised Mary greatly. She had never had an experience like this. Neither had she heard words like these. For that reason verse 29 says, "But she was greatly troubled at what was said and pondered what sort of greeting this might be." Without doubt she was thinking, *What's this? Is this angel really a messenger of God? Why is he saying that I am favored?*

Knowing that this was a new experience and that she had never heard these words, she did not close her mind but instead continued trying to understand the meaning of this. Instead of coming to the conclusion that it was all very strange, she continued searching for the truth. She maintained an open mind and heart.

Studying the Word of God we find teachings that will be new to us. In addition to this, we will feel the presence of God in our heart like we have not felt before. It is probable that, going through his Word, God will put in our heart a desire to draw closer to him, to know him better, or to change something in our life that does not please Him. So that this becomes a reality in our life, we need to follow the example of Mary and keep an open mind to the Word of God.

Mary Maintained a Receptive Faith

In verse 30 and 31 we find the message of the angel to Mary. "Then the angel said to her, Do not be afraid, Mary, for you have found favor with God. Behold, you will conceive in your womb and bear a son, and you shall name him Jesus." What the angel was saying seemed impossible. That is why Mary asked: "How can this be since I have no relations with a man?" (v. 34).

The act of Mary asking questions does not mean that she did not have faith. She did not express doubt nor did she ask for a sign like Zechariah. She did not doubt that God could do this. The only question that she had was how could this be? Her faith was a receptive faith. She did not understand all the details but was willing to learn.

Asking questions is not a sign of lack of faith. It is important that we understand the teachings of the Word of God. To achieve this we have to ask questions. There are people who say: "It is not important what we believe in as long as we have faith." That is a blind and dangerous faith that can deceive people. It is not enough to believe. It is important to know what you believe in. Solid faith is a faith that is based on the teaching and promises of God. But, to understand these teachings and these promises, we need to study God's word and ask questions. Throughout his ministry here on earth, our Lord Jesus Christ was never offended when people asked him sincere questions. He always took the time to answer them.

In these studies many questions are going to emerge. We should feel free to ask about that which we do not understand. At the same time, we should keep a receptive faith toward that which God wants to teach us and that which he wants to do in our life.

Mary Showed Admirable Submission

What the angel said to Mary was going to change her life completely. Having a child could cause her enormous problems.

What would people say knowing that she was pledged to be married, but was now pregnant? How would Joseph react? Would he reject her, thinking that she had been unfaithful? In addition to this, how prepared was she to accept the responsibility not only to give birth to the Son of God, but also to raise him and guide him until he grew and began his mission? Without doubt many questions flooded the mind of Mary.

The angel answered her questions when he told her: "for nothing is impossible for God" (v. 37). Upon hearing this, Mary said, "Behold, I am the handmaid of the Lord. May it be done to me according to your word" (v. 38). Mary showed marvelous obedience. She was willing to submit herself to the will of God. It did not matter to her how high the cost was; she was willing to obey the Word of God.

27

Mary's submission was admirable! She inspires us to search, to understand, and to obey the will of God.

Continuing this study of the Word of God, helps us to imitate this beautiful decision of Mary.

Let us think about the implications of this for our life and let us ask these questions:

Do I purpose to:

1. Have an open mind in order to learn valuable lessons from the Word of God?

2. Keep a receptive faith, knowing that although I don't understand everything, God will help me find the answers for my questions?

3. Maintain a humble submission to the will of God, knowing that he desires the best for me?

We conclude this beautiful lesson with The Lord's Prayer. Giving our special attention to the phrase: "Your will be done, on earth as in heaven" (Matthew 6:10).

Bible Memory Verse:

"She will bear a son and you are to name him Jesus, because he will save his people from their sins" (Matthew 1:21).

Prayer:

"Our Father who art in heaven hollowed be thy name; thy kingdom come; thy will be done on earth as it is in heaven. Give us this day our daily bread; and forgive us our trespasses as we forgive those who trespass against us. And lead us not into temptation; but deliver us from evil. Amen."

Dear God, please help me to have the faith and the submission to your will that the Virgin Mary had when she heard your message from the angel Gabriel. Thank you for hearing my prayer. Amen.

THE VISITATION OF MARY TO ELIZABETH
(Luke 1: 39-56)

The visitation of Mary with her cousin Elizabeth took place as a result of what the angel had told her. The angel that told Mary that she was going to give birth to the Son of God explained that this was going to be accomplished through a miracle. The birth of Jesus would be the result of the work of the Holy Spirit and not the result of a marital union with a human father. The angel said:

> "The Holy Spirit will come upon you, and the power
> of the Most High will overshadow you. Therefore the child
> to be born will be called holy, the Son of God" (Luke 1:35).

While Mary was still wondering how this miracle could be possible, the angel gave her information about another miracle that was already in the process of taking place. He said to her:

> "And, behold, Elizabeth, your relative, has also
> conceived a son in her old age, and this is the sixth month
> for her who was called barren; for nothing will be
> impossible for God" Luke 1:36,37.

The same angel, Gabriel, who announced to Mary that she would be the mother of the blessed Savior of the world, had appeared to Zacharias, a Jewish priest. Gabriel told Zacharias that his wife was going to have a son " who would prepare a people fit for the Lord" (Luke 1:1-17). What made this a miracle was that both Zacharias and Elizabeth were well advanced in years and beyond the normal child bearing stage in their lives (Luke 1:18). This information was given to Mary as proof that the same God who made it possible for Elizabeth to conceive in her old age was going to make it possible for her, as a virgin, to give birth to the Son of God (Luke 1:27).

After hearing this, Mary went "in haste" to the city of Judah to visit Elizabeth (v. 39). Her haste undoubtedly came from a desire to congratulate her cousin on the impending birth of her child. She wanted to see first hand evidence of the miracle that God was performing. Her greatest motivation for visiting Elizabeth, however, was to seek confirmation of her faith as pointed out by the angel.

She also wanted to receive encouragement and support from her cousin during a time of deep soul searching and transition in her life.

Elizabeth's Response to Mary's Visit (vv. 41-45)

From the very moment of Mary's arrival at her home, Elizabeth experienced several things that confirmed to her that something very special was about to happen.

The Babe Leaped in Elizabeth's Womb (v. 41)

This babe in Elizabeth's womb was going to be known as "John." He was going to have a very special mission. The angel had already told Zacharias:

> "And he will turn many of the children of Israel to the Lord their God. He will go before him in the spirit and power of Elijah to turn the hearts of fathers toward children and the disobedient to the understanding of the righteous, to prepare a people fit for the Lord "(Luke 1:16,17).

The mission of John the Baptist was going to be to prepare people to hear and respond to the message of Jesus, the Son of God. It is truly amazing to note that the babe who was in his sixth month of development within his mother's womb leaped upon hearing the voice of the one who was going to give birth to the Savior of the world. This was not a coincidence. The same God who was involved in the creation of John the Baptist was performing a miracle in Mary's womb so that a very special being with a blending of a divine and a human nature could come to this world to save us from our sins. In other words, in his infinite wisdom, God was coordinating these events so that there would be a person who would prepare the way for the ministry of his Son Jesus Christ, and this person was already showing excitement even though he had not been born yet. The unborn John the Baptist was already rendering homage to the Savior of the world.

Let's meditate:

1. Do we truly believe that God has the wisdom and the power to guide us in our daily lives?

2. If we do, what evidence do we have of this in the events that have taken place in our lives?

3. Could it be that this Bible Study itself may be used by God to draw us closer to him and to understand his plan for our lives?

Elizabeth was Filled with the Holy Spirit (v. 41)

Throughout the Bible, "being filled with the Holy Spirit", means that people experience God's presence in their lives. The expression was often used to describe the experience of the Old Testament prophets who would be filled with the presence of God and would be enabled to communicate God's message. For example, the prophet Isaiah was able to predict hundreds of years in advance that "the virgin shall be with child, and bear a son, and shall name him Immanuel" (Isaiah 7:14). Being filled with the Holy Spirit also resulted in receiving wisdom, strength, and boldness to live for God. Jesus said, "But when he comes, the Spirit of truth, he will guide you to all truth…" (John 16:13). When she was filled with the Holy Spirit, Elizabeth was enabled to understand what was happening in Mary's life and the significance of the baby that she was going to give birth to.

Let's meditate:

1. Does our religious experience consist mainly of knowing something about God and trying to live by a set of rules?

2. Are we experiencing the presence of God in our souls in such a way that we receive peace, comfort, guidance, and hope in our daily lives?

Elizabeth Acknowledged Mary's Blessing

Filled with the Holy Spirit, Elizabeth acknowledged the blessing that Mary had received from God: "Most blessed are you among women, and blessed is the fruit of your womb" (v.42). This was a way to express Mary's blessing in a superlative way. The meaning was "thou, most blessed woman!"

31

Mary's blessedness was that God chose her to be the mother of his Son. Elizabeth, filled with the Holy Spirit, acknowledged the fact that God had blessed Mary in a very special way.

She then explained why Mary had been blessed:

"Blessed are you who believe" (v. 45).

Mary had believed the message that the angel had given her. Even though the entire idea of a virgin giving birth was totally impossible from a human perspective and the thought that she had been chosen surprised her completely, she chose to believe God's message. The word that is used here for "believe" actually means, "to trust." Despite the surprising nature of the message, Mary trusted God with her life and her future.

Mary had been selected for a very special honor, but this honor carried with it a very heavy responsibility. She would give birth to a child even though she was not married. She could face the scorn and ridicule of people who did not understand. She would face many uncertainties regarding her son's mission, yet she believed. That's why Elizabeth called her blessed. Because Mary believed, she received God's blessing.

Let us meditate:

1. Jesus said, "But to those who did accept him he gave power to become children of God, to those who believe in his name" (John 1:12).

2. To believe in Jesus means to trust him with our lives and our eternal destiny. It means to receive him as our Savior because he is the only one who died for us.

3. Have we gone beyond knowing that Jesus exists to having a personal relationship of faith and trust in him?

Elizabeth Acknowledged God's Blessing on Jesus

In addition to acknowledging Mary's blessing, Elizabeth acknowledged that God's favor and concern were going to be upon Jesus forever. She said, "Blessed is the fruit of your womb" (v. 42). This was a reference to Jesus, who was going to be born after John the Baptist. Through faith, Elizabeth already celebrated the fact that Jesus was going to be born, even though there were no visible signs at that time that Mary was pregnant. She expressed complete confidence that the message of the angel was going to come true. She said, "Blessed are you who believed that what was spoken to you by the Lord would be fulfilled" (v.45). Elizabeth expressed confidence that God's ultimate goal communicated to Mary by the angel was going to be fulfilled in its entirety. It would start with the conception of Jesus and would continue through the life and ministry of the blessed Savior.

Elizabeth also gave evidence of her faith when she referred to Mary as "the mother of my Lord" (v. 43). Elizabeth had learned from experience that God was able to perform miracles and could be trusted to keep his promises. The evidence was in her own womb, for already she was six months pregnant with the child that had been promised to her and her husband. Elizabeth was also aware of the promise of a Savior that had been given to the people of God. She knew that the baby that was going to be born of the Virgin Mary was going to be her Savior and Lord.

Mary's Response to God's Favor (vv. 46 – 56)

Mary was undoubtedly touched by Elizabeth's response of joy and excitement regarding the news of future birth of Jesus. Elizabeth's faith had brought sweet comfort and assurance to her soul. Mary, however, was even more deeply touched by the way in which God had dealt with her and the significance of the life and ministry of the baby that she was going to give birth to.

Mary Praises God for Being Her Savior (vv. 46, 47)

Elizabeth's words had been directed to Mary. Mary's words, however, were directed to God. Elizabeth's words were a continuation of the angel's message to Mary. Mary's words were a continuation and expansion of her reply to the angel. Mary said: "My soul proclaims the greatness of the Lord." She praised God for all that he has done and rejoices in the salvation that will come to the world through the person of Jesus. Her praise came from her soul, the very depths of the life that animated her body.

Mary continued by saying, "My spirit rejoices in God my Savior." Mary not only magnified God and told of his greatness but rejoiced over the fact that salvation comes from him. A savior is one who rescues and delivers from mortal danger and places in a permanent state of safety. In saying these words, Mary gives evidence of the fact that she understood God's plan regarding the mission of Jesus as savior of the world.

Mary Praises God for Choosing Her (v. 48)

In addition to praising God for being her savior, Mary praised God for choosing her. She said:

"For He has looked upon his handmaid's lowliness."

Mary recognized the fact that she was not worthy of being God's instrument for the incarnation of his Son, Jesus. In Mary's mind, God could have chosen a person of high noble birth, a mighty queen, a daughter of a princes or even the daughter of a foremost religious leader in the nation of Israel. Instead, God chose a maidservant of lowly estate. Mary was very much aware of her humble condition. She had already demonstrated this awareness when she in response to the angel referred to herself as "the handmaid of the Lord" (v.38). She was astounded that despite her humble condition God had noticed and chosen her for such a glorious privilege. The fact that God looked with grace upon her lowly condition, also gives us great hope that he will look at our condition with grace, if we appear before him with a spirit of humility as Mary did.

Mary's amazement of having been chosen by God is reflected in her additional Statement, "behold, from now on will all ages call me blessed" (v.48). The idea that she would be seen as a person who had received God's favor did not originate with Mary. She was simply repeating what the angel had told her (see verse 28). Her secret was going to cease to be a secret. Her son would be born. He would step forth as the Savior of the world. All succeeding generations would know about him. In learning about his story, they would know that God had chosen a humble maiden to become the earthly mother of his Son Jesus Christ.

Let's meditate:

1. Do we have the spirit of humility that Mary demonstrated?

The Bible clearly teaches that it is only as we acknowledge our unworthiness that we are in a position to receive God's blessing of salvation. Jesus illustrated this spirit in the words of the prodigal son: "I have sinned against heaven and against you; I no longer deserve to be called your son" (Luke 15:21).

2. Are we following Mary's example of not focusing on herself, but pointing the attention of people toward God?

This is reflected in her statement:

"My soul proclaims the greatness of the Lord; my spirit
rejoices in God my savior (vv. 46, 47)."

Mary Praises God for the Great Things He Had Done (vv. 49-55)

In using the plural, Mary referred to the numerous things God had done.
These great things included choosing her, sending the angel, causing the
miraculous conception, and revealing these things to Elizabeth.

The "Mighty One" Did These Things

Mary acknowledged the fact that God is the one who posses the power
and ability to do these great things. The miracles that she was experiencing
could only come from God, the Mighty One. No one else could cause an
elderly woman to give birth, as was the case with Elizabeth, and no one else
could make it possible for a virgin to conceive a child as was her own case.
Further, no one, other than God himself, could bring about the incarnation of
the Savior of the world.

The "Holy One" Did These Things

Mary did not just see God as the "Mighty One," but also as the one
whose name is "holy." To say that God is holy means that he is the absolute
opposite of sin. There is absolutely nothing that is sinful in his nature and his
actions. The word "holiness" also means that God is separate and all others
who are holy are separated unto God. Mary referred to the words of the
angel, "The Holy Spirit will come upon you" and "the child to be born will
be called holy, the Son of God" (v. 35) when she speaks of the holiness of
God. Mary's conception was brought about by God's holy power; therefore,
Jesus was to be born a holy being, completely free from sin. Only the one
whose name is "holy" could accomplish this.

The "Merciful One" Did These Things

Because God is completely holy, he made possible the birth of the sinless
Savior of the world. This holiness of God, however, is accompanied by his
mercy. If God were only holy, he would not want to have anything to do with
our sinful world. It is his mercy, however, that moves him to have compassion
on us who are in misery as a result of our sin and guilt. God's mercy motivated

him to send his Son to save a lost and dying humanity. This mercy was not only shown during Mary's life. It extends "from generation to generation." This means that God's mercy is available to us today.

God's mercy is not applied to everyone. It is applied only to those "who fear him." To fear God is to be in awe of him, to recognize his majesty and greatness, and to treat him and his commandments with respect. It means to be so moved by God's power, holiness, love, and grace, that we honor and obey him with a deep sense of reverence. If we approach God in a spirit of reverence, we will experience his mercy and his forgiveness. Mary praises God for his mercy.

The "Just One" Did These Things

The one who is mighty, holy, and merciful is also just. God opposes the arrogant, the oppressors, and those placing their trust in their material possessions.

Mary then described God's actions that will take place toward those who do not have a spirit of humility and reverence toward God. "He has dispersed the arrogant of mind and heart." This refers to those who at the very core of their being (their heart) are arrogant, skeptical, haughty, believing that they know more than God does. God has scattered them because they have not had the humility to acknowledge God in their lives. The same is true for those who are in power (the potentates) who use their power to oppress people. God has thrown them down from their thrones. Also, the rich who place their trust in their possessions, God has "sent away empty." In other words, God has not listened to them and their lives are spiritually hollow.

In contrast to these, God has exalted the humble ones. Mary's own experience was a testimony to the fact that God blesses those who have a spirit of humility. Also, God has filled the hungry with good things. God's concern for those who are physically poor and destitute is certainly expressed. This also includes, however, God's concern for those who are hungry for a relationship with him. Those who are humble and recognize their need for God will receive his mercy.

Mary Praises God for Keeping His Promise to His People (v. 54)

Let's Meditate:

There is much that we can learn from Mary and her song of praise to God.

1. Mary praised God for his majesty, mercy, and mighty works. How can we follow her example and praise God for all that he has done in sending us his Son Jesus to save us from our sins?

2. Mary demonstrated a spirit of humility. She acknowledged that she was not worthy of God's blessing in choosing her to be the mother of his Son, Jesus. How can we demonstrate a spirit of humility in acknowledging that we are not worthy of God's forgiveness and blessings?

3. Mary did not focus attention on herself. She always pointed to God as the one worthy of worship and adoration. She started her song of praise with the words, "My soul proclaims the greatness of the Lord." How can we follow her example and focus our worship on God?

Bible Memory Verse:

"And Mary said: My soul proclaims the greatness of the Lord; my spirit rejoices in God my Savior" (Luke 1:46,47).

Prayer:

Dear God, along with Mary, I want to proclaim your greatness and I want to rejoice in the fact that you are my Savior. Amen.

THE NATIVITY OF JESUS
(Luke 2:1-20)

There is no more beautiful and more inspiring story than that of the birth of our Lord Jesus Christ. Each Christmas people try to represent this marvelous account through drama, chorale presentations, manger scenes, decorations, paintings, and many other ways. Considering all these efforts, nothing can communicate the significance of this glorious event better than the study of the Sacred Scriptures. There we find a clear and moving description about the birth in the manger, the message of the angels, the joy of the shepherds, and the homage of the Magi.

The Birth of Jesus (Luke 2:1-7)

The birth of Jesus is the culmination of a series of miracles. As we have already seen in the previous lesson, the appearance of the angel and the announcement that the virgin would give birth to a child were supernatural accounts. An additional miracle is that the place where Jesus was going to be born was announced 700 years before his birth. The prophet Micah had said, "But you, Bethlehem Ephraim, too small to be among the clans of Judah, from you shall come forth for me one who is to be ruler in Israel"(Micah 5:1). How would this prophecy be fulfilled, Mary and Joseph were not living in Bethlehem but instead in Nazareth? We find the answer in Luke 2:1-5.

We see in verses 1 through 3 that Augustus Caesar, the emperor of Rome, ordered that all were to be registered in the census. This census was taken to charge the taxes and to know who had come of age to serve in the Roman army. This was difficult for the people who had to return to their town of birth to be counted in the census. Verse 4 explains that Joseph, who was from the family of King David, had to go to Bethlehem. But he did not go alone, instead he went "to be enrolled with Mary, his betrothed, who was with child" (v. 5). It is interesting to note that God used this census so that our Lord Jesus was born in Bethlehem (the city where the palace of David had been).

Being there "the time came for her to have her child" (v. 6). Mary and Joseph had not planned to be in Bethlehem for the birth of the child Jesus. But in the providence of God, they were in such a historical and important city when the time for the birth arrived.

To arrive in that city, Joseph and Mary had to travel 90 miles. After their arrival they began to look for an inn. In comparison with the hotels of our day, the inns were very primitive. They simply provided a rustic space to sleep and to prepare their own food and a separate place to keep the animals. Because so many other people had arrived for the census, Joseph and Mary did not find a place in the inn and had to stay in the place where the animals were kept.

Many people talk about the place where they were born. Some were born in a hospital, other in their homes, but few were born in a place as humble as a stable surrounded by donkeys, sheep, and camels. This was no clean little bed and soft, warm little room decorated for the child Jesus, but rather, they laid him on the straw in the manger. Although we like to adorn the Nativity scene, we cannot escape the fact that the cradle of the Son of God was a manger where the animals ate. His desire to demonstrate the love of God to us was so great that he was willing to be born as the poorest of the poor.

I spite of the circumstances of the birth of the baby Jesus, without doubt there was a profound joy in the heart of Mary and of Joseph thinking that the message of the angel had been fulfilled. The Savior of the world had been born!

The Message of the Angels

The important and rich people of the city were too wrapped up in their business to realize the event that had taken place that night. The message of the birth was given to some shepherds "living in the fields and keeping the night watch over their flocks "(v. 8). The shepherds were not considered to be important people in the Jewish society of that time. The Jews that were considered very religious despised the poor shepherds because they did not perfectly follow the rules, customs, and ceremonies of Jewish law. In spite of this, the shepherds of the region of Bethlehem played an important role in the care of the sheep that were offered as sacrifices at the Jewish temple. It is probable that, upon taking the sheep to the temple, they had often heard the parts of the Bible that spoke about the Savior of the world that was going to come. Although they did not have much knowledge about their religion, they had simple and sincere hearts. They were chosen to hear the first announcement of the birth of the baby Jesus.

As we see in verses 9 though 22, an angel appeared to these shepherds. This angel was surrounded by the glory of God manifested in a brilliant way. As we can imagine upon seeing this, the shepherds were scared. But the angel calmed their fears by giving them the message of the arrival of Jesus. This message was of the utmost importance for various reasons.

A Message of Peace

First, it was a message of *peace*. The angel said to the shepherds, "Do not be afraid." Through his ministry Jesus preached a message of peace. Many repeated times he said to his disciples, "Do not let your hearts be troubled" (John 14:1). He also told them, "Peace I leave with you; my peace I give you. Not as the world gives do I give it to you. Do not let your hearts be troubled or afraid" (John 14:27). Because Jesus came to bring peace to our hearts, he was called the "Prince of Peace" (Isaiah 9:5). As we study the message of the angel to the shepherds, it is important that we ask ourselves:

1. Do I have peace in my heart?

2. If I die tonight, do I have peace in my heart that I am prepared to meet God?

3. What do I need to do to have peace?

A Message of Joy

Second, this message is a message of *joy*. The angel said to the shepherds, "Do not be afraid; for behold, I proclaim to you good news of great joy that will be for all the people" (v. 10). It was a message of joy because it brought the good news that Jesus had been born. It was also a message of great joy because it was for all the people. The shepherds, whom the religious leaders had excluded, were now included in the plan of God. This message "for all the people" also includes us. At times we feel that we are not worthy and we try to do something to obtain the favor and mercy of God. But the message of the angel assures us that God sent his Son to us to communicate to us that He loves us very much and wants us to accept his help and blessings. Again, upon studying this story, we should ask ourselves:

1. How much joy do I have in my heart?

2. Does my happiness depend on favorable circumstances?

3. Have I invited Christ to bring his joy to my heart?

Jesus came to bring joy to our life. Jesus said, "I have told you this so that my joy might be in you and your joy might be complete" (John 15: 11). He explained that this joy comes when we remain in Him and He in us (v. 4). This means that we have invited him to come into our heart and to guide our life.

A Message of Salvation

Third, this message is a message of *salvation*. The angel told the shepherds, "today in the city of David a Savior has been born for you who is Messiah and Lord" (v. 11). At that time many Jews were looking for a political savior that would free them from their sicknesses and their physical limitations. But the message of the angel was about a Savior that would free them from the slavery of sin and of death. Today there are also many that are looking for saviors - people that can free them for the things that enslave them and oppress them, such as wickedness or vices, fears, sicknesses, and the feeling of guilt. None of them can save like Jesus. Only Jesus can save us from our sins, from a life of confusion, without purpose and eternal condemnation. In the light of the angel's message, it is important that each one asks himself:

1. Have I received Jesus as my Savior?

2. Have I asked him to free me from the things that control my life?

The Sign of the Angel

The angel not only gave the shepards a message, but he also gave them a sign: "You will find an infant wrapped in swaddling clothes and lying in a manger" (v. 12). This angel was accompanied by a choir of angels that sang, "Glory to God in the highest, and on earth peace to those on whom his favor rests" (v.14). At that time it was a custom to pay singers that celebrated the birth of a child. It is beautiful to think that the child Jesus, who was born in such a poor environment, did not receive a serenade from earthly singers (as was the custom at that time), but instead a serenade of heavenly angels sent by the heavenly Father.

The Faith of the Shepherds

We should admire the faith of the shepherds. After having received the message of the angel, they did not spend time discussing whether what had happened was real or not. Immediately they decided to go to Bethlehem to see what had been reported to them (v. 15). We see in them an attitude similar to that of Mary. They believed and they obeyed.

Because of their simple faith they "found Mary and Joseph, and the infant lying in the manger" (v. 16). When the shepherds arrived at the manger and reported what they had seen and heard, without doubt the hearts of Mary and Joseph were filled with joy knowing the heavenly Father had entrusted them to announce the birth of Jesus. The shepherds, who were considered the most insignificant of all people, were also filled with joy for having the privilege of being the first to see Jesus (v. 20). In the Bible we find that, time after time, Jesus admired, not those that had the most religious knowledge, but rather those that had a sincere faith like that of the shepherds.

The Praise of the Shepherds

The birth of our Lord Jesus was a happy event. The angel told the shepherds that he brought "good news of great joy" (v. 10). The choir of angels joyfully sang, "glory to God in the Highest!" (v. 14). Upon arriving at the manger, the shepherds observed the profound joy in the hearts of Mary and Joseph. And after having seen the divine face of the baby Jesus, the shepherds "returned, glorifying and praising God" (v. 20).

The entire scene of the birth of Jesus is filled with joy. But there is a sad expression there, "and she wrapped him in swaddling clothes and laid him in a manger, because there was no room for them in the inn." (v. 7). It is sad that the Son of God had to be born among the animals because the humans did not give him a place in their homes. It is sad that this scene is repeated every day when people do not have a place in their hearts for Jesus. In the same way that Mary and Joseph went from door to door looking for a dwelling to give birth to the Son of God, Jesus is seeking a dwelling in our hearts. Jesus says, "Behold, I stand at the door and knock. If anyone hears my voice and opens the door, [then] I will enter his house and dine with him, and he with me" (Revelation 3:20).

How beautiful to think that, in a spiritual manner, we can invite Jesus to come to live in our heart and to accompany us in the long walk of life. This idea we find in the song that says:

> You left your throne and crown for me,
> To come to Bethlehem to be born;
> But to you no entrance to the inn was given
> And in the stable you were given birth.
> Come into my heart, O Christ!
> For in it there is a place for you;
> Come into my heart, O Christ! Come.
> For in it there is a place for you.

We too will receive the joy found in the song of the angels and the joy that the shepherds experienced if we invite Christ to come to live in our hearts.

Bible Memory Verse:

"Behold, I stand at the door and knock. If anyone hears my voice and opens the door, [then] I will enter his house and dine with him, and he with me" (Revelation 3:20).

Prayer:

Dear Jesus, it makes me sad to know that you had to be born in a manger because people were so busy and so involved in their own activities that they didn't have room for you. I invite you to come into my heart and guide me so that I may enjoy your presence and live for you. Thank you for hearing my prayer, Amen.

THE PRESENTATION OF JESUS IN THE TEMPLE
(Luke 2:21-38)

Christian couples know that the birth of a child has to be a gift from God. Thinking about the great privilege and the great responsibility they have assumed, they cannot help but dedicate themselves and dedicate their child to the Creator of the universe. This helps them to recognize that the child really belongs to God and that they need his help in raising him.

The people of God had a ceremony to dedicate their children to the Lord; the presentation in the temple. In order to have a better understanding of the presentation of Jesus in the temple we are going to see what Luke says about the presentation of Jesus in the temple, the meaning of the presentation, and the message in the presentation.

The Preparation for the Presentation

In the gospel of Luke we find a description of the preparation that took place before presenting a child in the temple.

The Preparation of the Child

Luke says,

> "When eight days were completed for his circumcision,
> he was named Jesus, the name given him by the angel before
> he was conceived in the womb" (2:21).

In accordance with the law of God for the Jewish people, males were circumcised on the eighth day. This was a sacred ceremony that indicated that the child was received as a member of the chosen people of God. Although Jesus, as the Son of God, did not have to be initiated into the people of God, he did this to fulfill the law of the Lord. The life of our Lord Jesus Christ was one of complete obedience to the heavenly Father. Jesus, who taught us to pray, "Your will be done, on earth as it is in heaven," began his life in obedience and ended it saying in the Garden of Gethsemani, "Father, if you are willing, take this cup away from me; still, not my will but yours be done" (Luke 22:42).

45

In addition to being integrated into the family of God, the child received his name during the ceremony of the circumcision. In the case of this child, they did not have to look for a name. The angel had already given him one, "you are to name him Jesus, because he will save his people from their sins" (Matthew 1:21). The name of Jesus indicated his mission. He came to save us from our sins. As we participate in this study it is important that we ask ourselves, has the mission of Jesus been completed in my life? Has he saved me from my sins?

The Preparation of the Mother

Luke adds:

> "When the days were completed for their purification according to the Law of Moses, they took him up to Jerusalem to present him to the Lord."

The preparation for the presentation included the purification of the mother. The law that God had given to Moses indicated that if a son was born, there had to be a period of one week for the purification of the mother and 33 days before she could enter into the temple (Leviticus 12:1-8).

In the ceremony of the purification the parents gave a lamb for a burnt offering and a turtledove for the expiation of sin. If the people did not have enough money to buy the lamb, they were permitted to bring two turtledoves or two doves (Leviticus 12:8). This was called the offering of the poor. This reveals that Jesus was raised in a poor home where they did not have any luxuries, where the meals were humble, and where they had to work hard to earn the daily bread. The Word of God explains why Jesus understands our situation, "for we do not have a high priest who is unable to sympathize with our weaknesses, but one who has similarly been tested in every way; "yet without sin" (Hebrews 4: 15). Because from his childhood Jesus knew what it was to experience hunger, thirst, cold, pain, anguish and anxiety, He can sympathize with us. For this reason we can cry out to him when we have a need. The Bible adds, "So let us confidently approach the throne of grace to receive mercy and to find grace for timely help"(Hebrews 4:16). Take this moment to meditate:

1. Am I suffering from something with which Christ can help me?

2. Do I have a worry that I need to put in the hands of Christ?

3. Do I have a feeling of guilt that I need Christ to forgive and take out of my life?

Take a moment right now to talk about it with Jesus in prayer, knowing that he understands your situation.

The Preparation of the Father

The Word of God teaches that Joseph was not the biological father of Jesus. The Son of God was born as a result of the work of the Holy Spirit. Joseph, nevertheless, was an instrument of God for providing a home in which Jesus could grow and prepare himself for the mission of his heavenly Father. Joseph, then, was present at the presentation of the baby, Jesus. In addition to this, he also purified himself for this solemn rite. Luke says, "when the days were completed for their purification according to the Law of Moses"(2:22), which implies that *Joseph* was also purified. What a beautiful example from this couple! They showed their obedience to the law of the Lord in all that they did.

The presentation of a baby included the dedication of the parents to follow God and to give the type of example to their son that honored the heavenly Father.

Let us take time to ask ourselves:

1. Have I dedicated myself to God so that my family will also be dedicated to Him?

2. Am I giving the type of example to my family that honors God and inspires them to draw close to Him?

The Meaning of the Presentation

Although they followed all the requirements prescribed by the law of the Lord, the presentation of Jesus was different from that of all the Hebrew children of that time. The nature of Jesus was different for he is the Son of

47

God. The mission of Jesus was different, for he came to this world with a special purpose.

As Saint Luke says:

> "Now there was a man in Jerusalem called Simeon, who was righteous and devout. He was waiting for the consolation of Israel, and the Holy Spirit was upon him. It had been revealed to him by the Holy Spirit that he would not die before he had seen the Lord's Christ" (2:25-26).

In these verses and in those that follow, Simeon describes the purpose for which Jesus came to this world.

Jesus Presented as the Consolation (v. 25)

The people of God had the hope that one day the Messiah would come and that his coming would be a solace (consolation) for them. Through his ministry, Jesus was a solace for afflicted persons. Bartimaeus, the blind man, cried out, "Jesus, Son of David, have pity on me!" (Luke 18:35-43). "Lord, if you had been here, my brother would not have died" were the words that were spoken to him by Mary, the sister of Lazarus (John 11:32). Upon hearing this, Jesus was moved in the spirit and "deeply troubled" (v.33) and later "Jesus wept" (v.35). But this was not the end. Jesus raised Lazarus to life again (v.44).

Jesus not only brought great solace to the people in that time, but also consoles us today through his Spirit. Before going to heaven, Jesus said to his disciples, "I will ask the Father, and he will give you another Advocate to be with you always" (John 14:16). By his Spirit, Jesus is with his followers each moment of our lives to give us consolation, peace, and direction. If there is grief in your life, if you have lost a loved one, if you feel sad, and disconsolate, invite Jesus to bring solace to your heart. Let us meditate on this right now:

1. Is there grief in my life that I need Christ to console?

2. Do I feel sadness from the loss of a relative?

3. Do I feel hopeless about a situation in my life?

4. Have I invited Christ to bring consolation to my life?

Jesus Presented as the Anointed of the Lord

Simeon had been promised, "he should not see death before he had seen the Messiah of the Lord" (Luke 2:26). At that time one put olive oil on the head of a person to dedicate him or her for a special work. The prophet Samuel, for example, anointed David to indicate that God had chosen him to be the king of Israel (1 Samuel 16:13). Jesus is presented here as the "Lord's Christ," which means that he was separated for a special mission. Jesus explained this when he began his ministry:

"The Spirit of the Lord is on me, because he has anointed me to bring glad tidings to the poor. He has sent me to proclaim liberty to captives and recovery of sight for the blind, to let the oppressed go free, and to proclaim a year acceptable to the Lord"(Luke 4:18-19).

Jesus Presented as the Salvation

Simeon continues, "for my eyes have seen your salvation" (v. 30). Jesus showed his understanding of his mission when he said, "the Son of Man has come to seek and to save what was lost" (Luke 19:10). To be lost means to not have a right relationship with God, living in a state of rebellion against God, not taking God into account in our life, permitting sin to control our life and not living in agreement with the purpose for which God created us.

To free us from this lost condition, Jesus came, died for our sins, rose the third day, and now is at the right hand of God interceding on our behalf. The salvation that Jesus offers us includes forgiveness of sins, freedom from the influence of Satan in our life, transformation of our character, the abiding presence of Christ in our heart, and the security that we will be with Him when we pass from this life into eternity.

In light of these truths it is important that we ask ourselves:

1. Have I asked Christ to forgive my sins?

2. Have I asked Christ to free me from the influence of Satan in my life?

3. Have I asked Christ to change my character?

49

4. Have I asked Christ to be with me every moment?

5. Have I asked Christ to give me the assurance that when I die, I will be with Him in heaven?

It is important for us to know that Jesus is the only Savior of humanity. Although there have been many pious and religious persons, none of them has been the Anointed One by God to save humanity. None of them has died for our sins and none of them has risen from the dead.

Jesus Presented as the Light for Revelation to the Gentiles

Simeon describes Jesus as the "light for revelation to the Gentiles" (Luke 2:32). The word *Gentiles* is used often in the Bible to refer to the nations of the world. This means that Jesus came to offer salvation to all the people of the world. There are people that feel excluded because they do not believe that they are worthy. The truth is that no human being merits God's favor. The word of God says,"all have sinned and are deprived of the glory of God" (Romans 3:23). None of us deserves the forgiveness and the favor of God. It is because of this that God made provision for us through his Son Jesus Christ. The Bible adds: "But God proves his love for us in that while we were still sinners Christ died for us" (Romans 5:8). Our part is not to try to do something good to obtain the favor of God, but rather to accept that which Christ has already done for us.

John writes of Jesus, "But to those who did accept him he gave power to become children of God, to those who believe on his name" (John 1:12). The question, then, with which we can conclude this beautiful study, is 'have I received Christ in my heart?'

Bible Memory Verse:

"But to those who did accept him he gave power to become children of God, to those who believe in his name" (John 1:12).

Prayer:

Dear Jesus, I thank you that you came to be a spiritual light for all of the people of the world. Help me to follow your light and to find peace with God, Amen.

THE FINDING IN THE TEMPLE
(Luke 2: 40-51)

After dedicating Jesus in the Temple, Joseph and Mary returned to Galilee. There Jesus "grew and became strong, filled with wisdom; and the favor of God was upon him" (v. 40). He grew up physically in the most normal way with nothing to deter his bodily development. He grew up mentally in the same way as he continued to attain strength of mind and wisdom. His development of mind and soul was unobstructed by any result of sin as he continued to absorb wisdom from God's word. Although his physical development was normal by human standards, his spiritual development, however, was vastly beyond those of mere human beings. This verse of Scripture makes it clear that Jesus went through the various stages of development in his bodily, mental, and spiritual life as a Divine Being clothed in human nature.

The Bible says that: "the favor of God was upon him" (v. 40). This means that Jesus was the recipient of God's favor in every aspect of his life. Because he was sinless, Jesus lived in the undimmed sunshine of God's blessed favor. His spiritual and mental qualities gave him the capacity to see through every error and deception. He possessed truth in its full measure and was able to master every situation. The experience of Jesus in the Temple in Jerusalem is like a snapshot that gives us a glimpse of how brilliant Jesus was and how, by the age of twelve, he had an understanding of his God-given mission on this earth.

Joseph and Mary Went to Jerusalem (v. 41)

Joseph and Mary went to the Jerusalem every year. The reason for the visit was to attend the Passover festival. It was expected that every Godly Jew should go to Jerusalem for this important and historical festival.

This festival commemorated the miracle that contributed to the liberation of the Hebrew people from Egypt. God had instructed Moses that every household should offer a lamb in sacrifice and "take some its blood and apply it to the two door posts and the lintel of every house in which they partake of the lamb" (Exodus 12:7). And God made a promise to the Hebrew saying: "Seeing the blood, I will pass over you; thus, when I strike the land of Egypt, no destructive blow will come upon you" (v. 13). The Egyptians, who were holding the Hebrews as slaves, and repeatedly refused God's command to let them go, received God's judgment and in one night, all of their firstborn were struck dead (v.29). This convinced Pharaoh to let the Hebrew people go (vv. 31,32). The Passover became a festival that the Hebrew people observed to commemorate God's deliverance from Egyptian slavery and to teach their children the significance of this event in the life of this nation.

The devotion of Joseph and Mary is demonstrated in the fact that they made the eighty-mile trip to Jerusalem every year to participate in this important festival. Luke 2:42 says: "and when he was twelve years old, they went up according to festival custom." The implication is that this was Jesus' first trip back to Jerusalem since he had been dedicated in the Temple. This was a special trip for them because at this age a Jewish boy was considered "a son of the law" and was expected to learn and observe its provisions.

Joseph and Mary Left Jerusalem (v. 43)

The Passover celebrations generally took seven days. It is obvious that they remained there for the entire time because verse 43 says: "as they were returning, the boy Jesus remained behind in Jerusalem, but his parents did not know it." At first glance it seems inexcusable that Joseph and Mary did not know that Jesus was not with them. The truth of the matter, however, is that people in these religious pilgrimages would usually travel in caravans. These caravans were composed of family members, friends, and other people from the same town or village who traveled with great religious enthusiasm and a genuine spirit of friendliness. Verse 44 explains: "Thinking that he was in the caravan, they journeyed for a day and looked for him among their relatives and acquaintances." Traveling an entire day on donkeys and on foot took much effort and energy. When they discovered, however, that Jesus was not in their caravan, they decided to go back to try to find him. Verse 45 says: "Not finding him, they returned to Jerusalem to look for him."

Jesus was Found in the Temple (v. 46)

Joseph and Mary were undoubtedly very worried about Jesus. To start with, they did not know where he was. They just knew that he was not with them. They must have searched all along the highway back to Jerusalem. When they got to the city, they searched everywhere. They very likely went back to the place where they had been lodging. It was not until the third day that they found him in the Temple. The temple was perhaps the place they least expected to find him. Most children his age would have found other children with whom to play or would have spent much time curiously looking at all of the interesting places in that large and historical city.

Jesus Listened to the Rabbis and Asked Questions

Verse 46 says: "After three days they found him in the temple, sitting in the midst of the teachers, listening to them and asking them questions." It was the custom of the Jewish teachers (rabbis) to teach groups that would gather in the Temple. The picture we get is one of Jesus sitting attentively listening to the teachings of these rabbis. He was well trained and knew how to show respect toward these rabbis. He listened attentively to them for he was intensely interested in all that they had to say, and compared what they said with the spiritual insights that he had gained from reading the teachings of the prophets in the local synagogues in Galilee. Jesus did not just listen but asked important questions. The questions that Jesus asked revealed that he had an interest and insights that were far beyond the normal level of learning and understanding of a twelve year old boy. The fact that he was sitting "in the midst" of them implies that he was given a place of honor by the doctors of the Law.

Jesus Answered the Rabbis' Questions

Verse 47 says: "And all who heard him were astounded at his understanding and his answers." There must have been a large group that gradually gathered to hear this amazing boy. They continued to be deeply impressed with his comments and answers. They truly wondered where that wisdom was coming from. The marvelous way in which Jesus demonstrated an ability to grasp and combine thoughts and reply to the questions that they put before him was absolutely mind-boggling to them. This was not just a very precocious child but his supernatural mind was filled with heavenly wisdom. He brought with him a clear knowledge of God's Word, in which no doubt he had been versed from earliest years and a mind and spirit undisturbed and unclouded by errors and fantastical interpretations that prevailed in the rabbis' schools of that day. This is why they were amazed by what he was saying.

Jesus Listened to His Parents' Concerns

Verse 48 says: "When his parents saw him, they were astonished, and his mother said to him, "Son, why have you done this to us? Your father and I have been looking for you with great anxiety."

Joseph and Mary were shocked to find Jesus in the temple surrounded by Rabbis who were learning from him. Up to this time, Jesus had not given evidence publicly of his nature and mission. There is no indication that he had spoken in a synagogue before. But now his parents find him in the most sacred place in Israel, the Temple itself, with prominent teachers focusing their attention on him and listening eagerly to his every word.

Mary's question reveals how deeply worried they had been about him for three days not knowing where he was or what might have happened to him. They had been searching for him "with great anxiety." Yet, despite her deep sense of anxiety, she addressed Jesus with tenderness. She started by calling him "Son" (literally in the Greek *teknon, a child*). At the same time she let him know how distressed they had been because they did not know where he was. Parents cannot blame Joseph and Mary for being so concerned about their child's disappearance for three days in that large city.

Jesus Responded to His Parents' Concerns

Jesus said to them: "Why were you looking for me? Did you not know that I must be in my Father house?" (v. 49)

These are the first recorded words of Jesus in the Bible. He responded in a calm and respectful way. The picture that we get here and throughout the Bible is that Jesus was always very respectful of his earthly parents (see verse 51). He, therefore, was not showing lack of respect in his reply. More that anything, Jesus was surprised that they did not know where he was and what he was doing. He assumed that they knew that he had to be involved in the things connected with his Father. Some translations state, "Did you not know that I must be in my Father's house?" In the original language (Greek), however, the statement is: "Did you not know that I must be about the affairs of my Father?" He was doing his Father's will in learning more about the teachings and practices at the Temple. He was also doing his Father's will by asking questions that would cause even the great teachers of that day to examine their beliefs and understanding of God.

Jesus' answer also gives evidence that he has a clear understanding of his nature (as God's only Son) and of his mission (to do the will of God's only Savior of the world). While he loved his earthly mother and stepfather dearly, Jesus made it clear that he had a divine calling and a unique relationship with his heavenly Father. Jesus affirmed his love and respect for his earthly family however; he made it clear that he had a higher loyalty toward his heavenly Father. The awareness of his supreme duty to God did not dim the light of his love for his earthly family. It is very clear, however, that Jesus put these second in importance to his relationship with God, who continued to be first in his life.

Let's meditate:

1. What place does Jesus occupy in our lives?

2. Are there times when loyalty toward our family gets in the way of our doing what Jesus wants us to do?

3. If so, what would Jesus want us to do?

It is important to note that Jesus also made it very clear who his father really is. He calls God *my* Father. Here as well as in other parts of Scripture, Jesus used the singular personal pronoun "*my*" to refer to his heavenly Father. At the age of twelve, Jesus knew that God was *his* Father in a way that he was not the Father to anyone else. Referring to Jesus as "the Word," Saint John explained Jesus' relationship with God the Father. He stated, "In the beginning was the Word, and the Word was with God, and the Word was God" (John 1:1). He then added, "And the Word became flesh and made his dwelling among us, and we saw his glory, the glory as of the Father's only Son, full of grace and truth" (1:14). These verses explain the divinity as well as the humanity of Jesus. He is divine because he is God's only Son. He is human because by being born of the Virgin Mary, he took on human form. This makes Jesus totally unique. There is absolutely no one like him. This is why only he can be the savior of the world. Jesus explained this when he said to Nicodemus: "For God so loved the world that he gave his only Son, so that everyone who believes in him might not perish but might have eternal life" (3:16). The Bible says: "There is no salvation through anyone else, nor is there any other name under heaven given to the human race by which we are to be saved" (Acts 4:12).

Let's meditate:

1. Are we aware that there is absolutely no one else like Jesus in the whole universe?

2. What does it mean to us that He is the only divine being who took on human form?

3. Does this mean that by having a human nature he can understand and sympathize with us?

4. Does this mean that by having a divine nature he can liberate us from our sins and change our lives?

Jesus' Parents Did Not Understand Him

The Bible states: "But they did not understand what he said to them" (v.50). When we read this, we can be tempted to ask: "Why did Mary not understand what Jesus said about his unique relationship to God and about his divine mission?" Didn't the angel tell Mary and Joseph that Jesus was going to be born as a result of God's direct intervention? Didn't the angel say to Mary that Jesus would be called the "Son of the Most High" (Luke 1:32) and "the Son of God" (Luke 1:35)? The answer to these questions is affirmative. The fact remains, however, that Jesus' parents did not fully understand the implications of the divinity of Jesus and of his mission as savior of the world. Mary's faith in particular is to be commended for continuing to trust God. She did not have a complete picture of all that was going to take place in the life of Jesus, yet she never ceased to be open to the will of God.

Let's meditate:

1. Are there some things about Jesus that we do not fully understand?

2. Are we willing to acknowledge that Jesus is the Son of God?

3. Are we willing to continue to learn about him and place our faith in him?

Bible Memory Verse:

For, if you confess with your mouth that Jesus is Lord and believe in your heart that God raised him from the dead, you will be saved" (Romans 10:9).

Prayer:

Dear Heavenly Father, Thank you for sending your Son Jesus to earth, to die on the cross, and to be raised from the dead. I am willing to confess that Jesus is my Lord and my Savior. Thank you for hearing my prayer, Amen.

PART TWO:

THE LUMINOUS MYSTERIES

In his Apostolic Letter, John Paul II explained his reasons for adding the *Mysteries of Light* to the Rosary:

> Of the mysteries of Christ's life, only a few are indicated by the Rosary in the form that has become generally established with the seal of the Church's approval. The selection was determined by the origin of the prayer, which was based on the number 150, the number of Psalms in the Psalter. I believe, however, that to bring out fully the Christological depth of the Rosary, it would be suitable to make an addition to the traditional pattern which, while left to the freedom of individuals and communities, could broaden it to include *the mysteries of Christ's public ministry between his Baptism and his Passion.*
>
> In the course of those mysteries we contemplate important aspects of the person of Christ as the definitive revelation of God. Declared the beloved Son of the Father at Baptism in the Jordan, Christ is the one who announces the coming of the Kingdom, bears witness to it in his works, and proclaims its demands. It is during the years of public ministry that *the mystery of Christ is most evidently a mystery of light*: "While I am in the world, I am the light of the world" (John 9:5).

Consequently, for the Rosary to become more fully a "compendium of the Gospel," it is fitting to add, following reflection on the Incarnation and the hidden life of Christ (the *joyful mysteries*) and before focusing on the suffering of his Passion (the *sorrowful mysteries*) and the triumph of the Resurrection (the *glorious mysteries*) a meditation of certain particularly significant moments in his public ministry (the *mysteries of light*).[1]

The *Luminous Mysteries* include: the baptism of Jesus in the Jordan (Luke 3:1-22), the self-manifestation at the wedding in Cana (John 2:1-11), the proclamation of the kingdom of God (Mark 1:15; 2:3-13), the transfiguration of Jesus (Luke 9:28-36), the institution of the eucharist (Luke 22:7-20).

[1]   John Paul II, *Apostolic Letter Rosarium Virginis Mariae*
      http://www.vatican.va/holy_father/john_paul_ii/apost_letters/documents/hf_jp-
      ii_apl_20021016_rosarium-virginis-mariae_en.html

THE BAPTISM OF JESUS
(Luke 3:1-22)

In the previous lessons we have studied the announcement of the birth of Jesus, the birth of Jesus, and the presentation in the temple. All these events help us to understand that Jesus is truly the Son of God. As the apostle John says, "And the Word became flesh and made his dwelling among us, and we saw his glory, the glory as of the Father's only Son, full of grace and truth."(John 1:14). The baptism of Jesus was another of the events that God used to help us to understand better the character and the ministry of our Lord Jesus Christ.[1]

The baptism of the Lord Jesus Christ is different than all the other baptisms that have been celebrated through the ages. This baptism was different because the one that baptized Jesus was different than all the other religious leaders. The message of the one that baptized Jesus was different than that of the other religious leaders. The mission of Jesus was explained in a clear way and the presence of God was manifested in a significant way. In Luke chapter 3 we find a beautiful description of the baptism of Jesus.

The Person who Baptized Jesus (Luke 3:1-6)

The Date on which John the Baptist Appeared

> "In the fifteenth year of the reign of Tiberius Caesar, when Pontius Pilate was governor of Judea, and Herod was tetrarch of Galilee, and his brother Philip tetrarch of the region of Ituraea and Trachonitis, and Lysanias was tetrarch of Abilene, during the high priesthood of Annas and Caiaphas . . ." (Luke 3:1-2).

Luke took much care in giving the exact date on which John the Baptist appeared to baptize Jesus. There are many writings of false religions that are the product of the human imagination. At times in these writings are found fictitious persons and events that in reality never occurred. In order to make it very clear that he is writing about a person that truly existed in human history, Luke tells who are the political and religious leaders in that time.

---

[1] The baptism of Jesus is not typically included in the Mysteries of the Rosary, however, this inspired portion of the Word of God is very important because it contains a direct testimony from God regarding the person and ministry of His Son.

The Work that was Given to John the Baptist

Verses 4 to 6 of this chapter of Luke explain the work that was given to John the Baptist:

> "Prepare the way of the Lord, make straight his paths. Every valley shall be filled and every mountain and hill made low. The winding roads shall be made straight, and the rough ways made smooth, and all flesh shall see the salvation of God."

In that time there were few roads. When a king went to visit a city, it was necessary to prepare the road. At times the workers of the city were used to do this. On other occasions the army was used. Their work included straightening the roads, smoothing the rough places and filling the low places so that the king could walk with ease and comfort.

The work of John the Baptist was to prepare the spiritual road for the coming of the King Jesus. The true Messiah (Christ) was different from the one who the Jews had been waiting for. They were waiting for a political liberator who would take vengeance on those that had been oppressing the Jewish people. To prepare the road, John had to guide them towards a spiritual reformation in mind, heart, and character. He had to help them form another concept so that they would accept Jesus as a reformer and the spiritual liberator. Jesus came to free them from the slavery of their sins and to change their life in such a way that they could find peace with God.

Thinking about the fact that John had to try to change the concept that they had about Jesus, it is important that we ask ourselves, 'what concept do I have about Jesus?' There are some people that think of Jesus as only a baby, "the holy child", in the arms of his mother. Others have a concept of Jesus as only the crucified Christ.

Let us take a moment to ask the question, what concept do I have about Jesus Christ?

1. As a baby in the arms of his mother?

2. As a dead man on the cross?

3. As being so holy that he does not want to come near to us?

4. As a Christ who arose from the dead?

5. As a Christ that is at the side of the throne of God pleading on my behalf?

6. As a Christ that is going to return for those who believe in Him?

Although the first two concepts are very moving, it is important that we accept the entire biblical concept about Jesus. It is true that Jesus came as a beautiful baby, but it is also true that this baby grew and fulfilled his mission of saving humanity. It is true that our Lord Jesus died a painful death on the cross, but it is also true that he rose from the dead and that he can live in our heart if we invite him. It is true that he went up to heaven, but it is also true that he is seated at the right hand of God to intercede for us. If Christ does not live in our heart and we do not feel his presence and his direction each day, then the mission with which He came has not been fulfilled in our life.

In verse 6 we find the purpose of John in preparing the way, "and all flesh shall see the salvation of God." In the Sacred Scriptures the word *salvation* means that we are freed from the slavery, the guilt, and the condemnation of the sin so as to have a relationship of love, companionship, peace, and hope with God (Luke 19:10, Romans 5:1).

The Message that John the Baptist Preached

The Message of John the Baptist is One of Judgment

John said to the crowds coming out to be baptized by him, "You brood of vipers! Who warned you to flee from the coming wrath?" (v. 7).

At first glance it seemed that the people had been receiving the message of John the Baptist and that as a demonstration of this they had been arranging to be baptized. The truth was that they had seen baptism as a talisman (something that could bring them good luck or would give them special favor). They believed that if they received the rite of baptism, they could avoid the punishment of God. John the Baptist knew what was in their hearts and he made them see that without an internal change, an external ritual would not have any merit before God. It is important, then, that we ask ourselves:

1. Am I depending on external religious rites to receive the favor of God without having had a change in my heart?

2. Do I think of my religious practices as a way to escape the punishment of God?

3. Do I feel motivated to come near to God through a feeling of fear instead of one of love?

The Message of John the Baptist is One of Repentance

"Produce good fruits as evidence of your repentance; and do not begin to say to yourselves, 'We have Abraham as our father,' for I tell you, God can raise up children to Abraham from these stones" (v. 8).

John the Baptist tells them: ***Show with your life that your repentance is true.*** The word ***repentance*** means that we are walking in one direction and afterwards we walk in the opposite direction. Not only do we feel regret for what we have done, but we ask God for forgiveness and we permit Him to change us in such a way that the entire direction of our life changes also. Let us ask ourselves:

1. Do I truly feel sadness for the way in which I have offended God with my actions?

2. Am I willing to confess my sins to God?

3. Am I willing to permit God to change the direction of my life? Is this what repentance means?

The Jews, especially the Pharisees, believed that because they were descendants of Abraham, they could live as they wanted to and still have the right to receive the blessings of the Messiah. John the Baptist tried to make them see that they should not depend on their religious traditions to free them from the punishment of God. If they did not repent and were not living lives that pleased God, the fact that Abraham was their ancestor was not going to help them in any way on the day of judgment. This makes us ask ourselves:

1. Are we counting on the fact that our parents were religious people to automatically make us recipients of the favor of God?

2. Do we believe that the religious tradition of our family is going to assure us that we are going to go to heaven?

3. Someone has said, "God does not have grandchildren only children." Is our personal relationship with God what we depend on?

The Baptism of Jesus

The baptism of the Lord Jesus Christ was different from that of all other human beings. It was different as much for it's meaning as for the special way in which God gave his approval.

The Meaning of the Baptism of Jesus

There are people who ask, why was Jesus baptized? He did not commit sin. Those who ask this question are right, because the Bible says clearly that Christ did not commit sin (Hebrews 4:15). If he did not commit sin, then why was he baptized? In the Word of God we find two reasons. First, the baptism was an act of obedience. Matthew explains that at first John the Baptist did not want to baptize Jesus, for he said: "I need to be baptized by you, and yet you are coming to me?" But Jesus answered, "Allow it now, for thus it is fitting for us to fulfill all righteousness"(Matthew 3:14-15). By being baptized, Jesus was showing his obedience to God. Second, the baptism of Jesus marked the beginning of his ministry. From childhood Jesus was preparing himself to complete his mission. After being baptized, Jesus began his ministry.

The Divine Testimony About Jesus

The baptism of Jesus was also different because God revealed himself in a special way at this event. Luke says:

"After all the people had been baptized and Jesus also had been baptized and was praying, heaven was opened and the Holy Spirit descended upon him in bodily form like a dove. And a voice came from heaven, 'You are my beloved Son; with you I am well pleased.'" (3:21-22).

At this event we see clearly the presence of the Holy Trinity. First we see the presence of the Holy Spirit in the form of a dove. The Holy Spirit the third

63

person of the Trinity came from heaven to anoint Jesus for his mission. Second, the voice that came from heaven was the voice of God, the Father. Third, Jesus, the beloved Son in whom God is pleased, is the second person of the Holy Trinity; Father, Son and Holy Spirit. Many prophets and religious leaders had come, but not one was the beloved Son of God. In Jesus we see the second person of the Trinity.

There are two important lessons that we learn from the baptism of Jesus. First, the Holy Trinity occupies the highest place in the Sacred Scriptures. God the Father, God the Son, and God the Holy Spirit is the One whom we should worship. Jesus affirmed this when he said, "The Lord, your God, shall you worship and him alone shall you serve" (Matthew 4:10). There are people in the Bible whom we admire greatly, but we should not worship them. Peter, for example, did not permit himself to be worshipped. He told Cornelius, who was prostrated, at his feet worshiping him to: "Get up. I myself am also a human being."(Acts 10:25-26). This should guide us to ask ourselves:

1. Am I giving God the first place in my life?

2. Am I reserving my worship for God the Father, God the Son, and God the Holy Spirit alone?

Second, believing that Jesus is the Son of God is absolutely necessary for our salvation. There are people who believe that Jesus was only a teacher, a prophet, a social reformer or a moral leader. Although it is true that Jesus was all of these, if we do not believe in Jesus as the Son of God we will not receive eternal salvation. John affirms this when he says:

> "Whoever believes in the Son of God has this testimony within himself. Whoever does not believe God has made him a liar by not believing the testimony God has given about his Son. And this is the testimony: God gave us eternal life, and this life is in his Son. Whoever possesses the Son has life; whoever does not possess the Son of God does not have life" (I John 5:10-12).

Having the Son is more than simply believing that He exists, knowing that he was born of the Virgin Mary, or affirming that he died on the cross. Having the Son means asking him to forgive our sins, receiving him in our heart as our personal Savior, and giving him the control of our life. Have you had this experience?

Let us ask ourselves:

1. What does Christ mean to me?

    a. Only a teacher?

    b. A prophet?

    c. A social reformer?

    d. A moral leader?

2. Having the Son means:

    a. Believing that He exists and that He is the Son of God, a person of the Trinity

    b. Knowing that He was born of the Virgin Mary

    c. Affirming that He died on the cross

    d. Asking him to forgive our sins

    e. Receiving him in our heart as our personal Savior

    f. Giving him control of our life

Bible Memory Verse:

"And the Word became flesh and made his dwelling among us, and we saw his glory, the glory as of the Father's only Son, full of grace and truth ' (John 1:14).

Prayer:

Dear Heavenly Father, help me to know what it means to have the living presence of your Son, Jesus Christ in my heart. It is in Jesus' name that I pray, Amen.

JESUS' SELF-MANIFESTATION AT THE WEDDING OF CANA
(John 2:1-12)

The first recorded miracle of Jesus took place at the beginning of his public ministry. On the two previous days, six men had become followers of Jesus (see John 1: 35-51). The performance of this miracle revealed the personality and power of Jesus as the Son of God. It confirmed the testimony that John the Baptist had said about him two days before: "Behold, the Lamb of God, who takes away the sin of the world" (John 1:29). There is much that we can learn about the nature and mission of Jesus as we study and reflect on the Biblical description of this event.

The Setting (John 2:1, 2)

Cana of Galilee was a small village near Nazareth. The scene of this event is a Jewish wedding feast. In accordance with Jewish custom, the bride and the groom were pledged to one another. It was not until after the wedding ceremony that they began to live as man and wife. Generally the groom and his companions brought the bride and her companions to the groom's home and began as grand a celebration as they could afford.

William Barclay describes a typical Jewish wedding feast:

> In Palestine the wedding festivities lasted for more than a day. The wedding ceremony itself took place in the evening after a feast. By that time it would be dark and they went through the village streets with the light of flaming torches and with a canopy over their heads. They were taken by as long a road as possible so that as many people as possible would have the opportunity to wish them well. But in Palestine a newly married couple did not go away for their honeymoon; they stayed at home; and for a week they kept open house. They wore crowns and dressed in their bridal robes. They were treated like a king and a queen. In a life where there was much poverty and constant hard work, this week of festivity and joy was one of the supreme occasions of life.[1]

John states that the mother of Jesus was at the wedding (2:1). The statement that she "was there" implies that she was more than an invited guest. She may have been related to one of the bridal couple or at least a close friend of the family.[2] This explains why she was privy to the information that the wine had run out and why she felt at liberty to instruct the waiters as to what they should do.

Jesus was a formally invited guest at the wedding (v. 2). He accepted the invitation and attended the wedding along with his disciples (v. 2). The fact that he was present at a wedding at the start of his public ministry is very significant. He was still in the process of choosing his disciples. A much larger city and a much more prominent setting could have been chosen for the launching of his ministry. Yet, he chose to spend time with what was obviously a very humble couple in a small village. The ministry of Jesus would later reiterate Jesus' commitment to the family and to humble people who turn to him in faith. It is important to point out that the love of Jesus and his concern for needy people is evident from the very beginning of his ministry. His first recorded miracle was performed in such a way as to spare the groom and the bride the terrible embarrassment of running out of provisions and not offering the type of hospitality that was expected of them.

Let's meditate:

1. Do we believe that Jesus is still concerned about people whom others might consider insignificant?

2. Do we believe that Jesus is interested in being with us in the different situations of our life?

3. Do we believe that Jesus is willing to help us even when we have made mistakes or failed to live up to our ideals?

The Crisis (John 2:3)

As has been pointed out, weddings were "supreme occasions" in the lives of people. Hospitality was considered a sacred duty in that culture. For provisions to fail at a wedding would be a terrible shame for the bride and the groom. That would have been humiliating.[3]

Knowing the situation in which this young couple was and feeling a deep sense of sympathy for them, Mary went to Jesus and told him: "They have no more wine" (v. 3). There are several interpretations as to the things that might have been in Mary's mind when she shared with Jesus information about the unfortunate crisis that the couple was facing. Was Mary merely communicating her anxiety about this potentially embarrassing situation to Jesus? Did she do so in the hope that Jesus might find a way to help this couple? Did she do so with the expectation that he would perform a miracle and save the day for this family? [4] On the basis of the information that is provided in this biblical passage, it is difficult to know precisely what it was that she had in mind. Was it any of these three reasons or perhaps a combination of them? We are not completely sure of what was on her mind when she shared this information with Jesus. What we do know is that she turned to the right person.

Lets' meditate:

In the Gospels we find numerous instances in which Jesus invites people with needs to turn to him.

"Come to me, all you who labor and are burdened, and I will give you rest" (Matthew 11:28).

"I will not reject anyone who comes to me" (John 6:37).

1. Are we turning to Jesus for answers to the deepest questions of life?

2. Are we seeking in him a sense of peace and assurance about our future?

3. Do we go to him when we face problems and crises in our lives?

4. We need to follow Mary's example and turn in faith to Jesus.

The Response (John 2:4)

While it is difficult to ascertain precisely what Mary had in mind when she uttered these words to Jesus, it is clear that Jesus viewed this as a form of request. He responded by saying: "How does your concern affect me?"

Read from the perspective of the 21st century, these words are difficult to understand. Perhaps the comments of Pope John Paul II in his Apostolic Letter can provide a framework from which to understand these words more fully. Commenting on the response of Mary and Joseph to Jesus' comments when he was found at the Temple ("I had to be in my Father's house"), the Pope states:

> The revelation of his mystery as the Son wholly dedicated to his Father's affairs proclaims the radical nature of the Gospel in which even the closest of human relationships are challenged by the absolute demands of the Kingdom. Mary and Joseph, fearful and anxious, "did not understand his words" (Luke 2:50).[5]

The expression "How does your concern affect me?" needs further clarification. In Greek (*ti emoi kai soi, gunai*) literally means "what to me and to you, woman?" It is an idiomatic expression that can be translated: "this is my concern, not yours." Barclay translates it: "Don't worry; you don't quite understand what is going on; leave things to me, and I will settle them in my own way."

Jesus then states: "My hour has not yet come." This expression is similar to the one he had used at the Temple "I must be in my Father's house." The thought that he conveys is that it is God who determines what he is going to do and when he is going to do it. The two expressions "woman" and "How does your concern affect me" coupled with the words "my hour has not yet come " combine to convey the thought that at this point in his ministry Jesus needed to establish fact that he is the Lord and Savior of all. He was not slighting his mother, whom he loved dearly, but he felt it necessary to point out to her that his instructions came from God, his heavenly Father. In other words, his common earthly relation must become secondary to the divine relation in the carrying out of his saving mission (Matthew 12:46-50).

The Gospel of John seeks to direct the attention of the readers to Jesus. From the very beginning, John establishes the fact that biological ties had to yield to the divine ties in Jesus' life and ministry. The fact that John refers to Mary as "the mother of Jesus" in this episode speaks of the necessity for John to identify just what relationship is being challenged and what authority is being established.[6]

What was Mary's response to Jesus' clarification? She told the men: "Do whatever he tells you" (v.5). Mary did not tell Jesus what to do, nor did she tell the men that she would get Jesus to do what she felt needed to be done. Instead, she pointed the men to Jesus and instructed them to follow his instructions. In other words, whatever he decides to do, it will be according to his will.

> Carson states: "In short, in 2:3 Mary approaches Jesus
> as his mother, and he clarifies her role; and in 2:5, she
> responds as a believer, and her faith is honored,"[7]

This presents Mary as a devoted follower of Jesus who continued to learn progressively as time went on about his divine nature and mission. In this passage Mary is portrayed as a consecrated and growing disciple who was still struggling to understand the ministry of Jesus. The clear meaning of the passage teaches that we should follow Mary's instructions: "Do whatever he tells you." As McCarthy points out, "these are Mary's last recorded words in the Scriptures. They stand as excellent advice for anyone seeking to please God."[8] Mary deserves our appreciation and love as well as our most sincere recognition that she was a pious woman, humble and full of faith, and that she was chosen by God to carry in her womb the redeemer of the world. Therefore, as was said by the angel when he announced to her the privilege, which God had given her, she will always be called blessed by all generations. The best way to honor Mary is to obey what she told the people at Cana "do whatever he [Jesus] tells you" (John 2:5).

Let's meditate:

1. Are we emulating Mary's example of faith and submission to Christ's will even when we do not know in advance how this is going to affect our lives?

2. Are we following Mary's advice: "Do whatever he tells you"?

3. What Jesus tells us in the Bible is: "I am the way and the truth and the life. No one comes to the Father except through me" (John 14:6). Are we willing to turn to him as our Lord and Savior?

The Miracle (vv. 6-10)

After recording the words spoken by Mary (do whatever he tells you), attention is focused on the water jars. "Now there were six stone water jars there for Jewish ceremonial washings each holding twenty to thirty gallons." This would make a total of up to one hundred fifty gallons. According to Jewish custom, the water was used for ceremonial washing of hands prior to participating in a meal. The implication is that the water in them had been used. This is consistent with the statement that there were a large number of guests at this wedding feast.

71

Jesus then told the waiters to "fill the jars with water". And they "filled them to the brim" (v. 7). It is important to note that it was the waiters and not the disciples that were instructed to fill the jars. This avoided any suspicion of collusion between Jesus and his disciples. The disciples had nothing to do with this. We have to admire the waiters for carrying out Jesus' orders. They may have wondered, "What is this Rabbi going to do with this water?" They may have thought, "Surely he is not going to serve them water hoping to get them to think that it is wine." Instead of spending their time wondering what Jesus was going to do, they obeyed his orders, "at once".

After the waiters had done what Jesus told them to do, Jesus gave them a second order: "Draw some out now and take it to the headwaiter" (v. 7). Once again, without questioning, the waiters carried out the instructions of Jesus. The verse says: "So they took it."

The waiter in charge was the manager of the feast. In addition to ensuring that all of the food and drink were there and were served properly, the waiter in charge had the responsibility of tasting the food and drink before they were offered to the guests.

The miracle that Jesus had performed was confirmed. Verse 9 and 10 states: "And when the headwaiter tasted the water that had become wine, without knowing where it came from (although the servers who had drawn the water knew), the headwaiter called the bridegroom and said to him, 'Everyone serves good wine first, and then when people have drunk freely, an inferior one; but you have kept the good wine until now'.

Busy in his activities, the waiter in charge had not noticed what had gone on elsewhere. The waiters did not speak because it took them a while to fully realize that they had just seen a miracle take place before their own eyes.

The waiter in charge thought that the groom had made a mistake by reserving the best wine for last. The groom himself was astonished until he realized that Jesus had turned the water into wine.

The Results (v. 11)

The description of this miracle concludes with the words; "Jesus did this as the beginning of his signs in Cana in Galilee and so revealed his glory, and his disciples began to believe in him."

St. John emphasizes the fact that Jesus performed his first miracle in "Cana of Galilee." Galilee was not the most prominent religious center; Judea was. In fact, there was a prejudice among the Jews about Galilee. They often said, "No prophet arises from Galilee" (John 7:52). It is important to note that Jesus did not focus on religion but on relationship. Often it was the religious traditions of the Jewish people (especially the Pharisees) that kept people from responding in faith to Jesus. Jesus was always willing to reveal himself and his power to those who sought him with a spirit of humility and repentance.

John calls these miracles "signs." The word "signs" point beyond themselves to something, which they accredit and attest.[9] These signs attest, first of all, to the person who works these signs and his significance. They give a strong and tangible testimony of the divinity of Jesus. They prove that Jesus is the only-begotten Son of God.

In addition to proving that Jesus is the Son of God, these signs (miracles) "manifested his glory." The purpose of these signs was to exhibit the presence and power of God in the life of Jesus. They are like a finger pointed toward God. They point to the greatness of God. They do not call attention to the persons who have been the recipients of the miracles (e.g., the groom), or even in some way participants in them (e.g., the waiters), but to the one who has worked the miracle (Jesus) and the one in whose power he has done it (God). The miracles that Jesus performs are not ends in themselves, but means to the ends. The purpose of Jesus' miracles is to draw people to God.

The miracle that Jesus performed accomplished its purpose. In chapter 1, we read that Andrew, John, James, Peter, Philip, and Nathaniel had become followers of Jesus (see John 1: 35-51). In chapter 2, verse 11, we read: "And his disciples believed in him." Initially, these men were inquirers. Two of them who were disciples of John the Baptist got near to Jesus and he asked them: "What are you looking for" (John 1:38). The next day Philip spoke to Nathanael about Jesus and he asked: "Can anything good come from Nazareth?" (John 1:46) These men, therefore, had been attracted by the teachings of Jesus and were in the process of learning more about him. After they saw the miracle they "believed in him." The startling evidence of the divine Messianic power and dignity of Jesus strengthened them in their belief. They accepted him as their personal Lord and Savior.

Let's Meditate:

1. Jesus performed a miracle in Galilee because the waiters had an attitude of humility and openness. Do we have this type of attitude when it comes to learning more about Jesus and wanting to relate to him more closely?

2. The waiters did not fully understand what Jesus was about to do, but they followed his instructions trusting that he knew what he was doing. As a result of this, they were participants in the miracle that Jesus performed. Are we willing to put our faith in Jesus even though we do not fully understand all of his teachings in advance?

3. Jesus' miracles were performed with the purpose of revealing his character and his will for those who were the recipients. Are we willing to look for evidence of the presence and purpose of Jesus in the miracles that we experience in our lives and in the lives of those around us?

4. St. John says that, after seeing the miracle, the disciples believed in him. This means that they placed their trust, their lives, and their future in the hands of Jesus. It means that they came to have a personal relationship with Jesus. They did not just know *about him*, they *knew him* in a personal way. Have we arrived at the point where we have a personal relationship with Jesus Christ?

Bible Memory Verse:

"But these are written that you may [come to] believe that Jesus is the Messiah, the Son of God, and that through this belief you may have life in his name" (John 20:31)."

Prayer:

Dear Jesus, just as you performed the miracle of changing the water into wine, I pray that you will change my life so that it will honor you and be a blessing to many people. Thank you for hearing my prayer, Amen.

End Notes

[1]   William Barclay, *Daily Bible Study: The Gospel of John*, (Philadelphia: Westminster Press, 1956), 81, 82.

[2]   See RCH Lenski, *The Interpretation of St. John's Gospel*, (Minneapolis: Augsburg Publishing House, 1961), 185.

[3]   William Barclay, *Daily Bible Study: The Gospel of John*, (Philadelphia: Westminster Press, 1956), 82.

[4]   For a discussion of these options see Stephen Hartdegen, "The Marian Significance of Cana," *Marian Studies II* (1960), 87-88, cited in Eric D. Svendsen, *Who Is My Mother* (Amityville, NY: Calvary Press, 2001), 175.

[5]   John Paul II, *Apostolic Letter, 10.* http://www.vatican.va/holy_father/john_paul_ii/apost_letters/documents/hf_jp-ii_apl_20021016_rosarium-virginis-mariae_en.html

[6]   Svendsen, op. cit., 190.

[7]   D. A. Carson, "John," *The Expositor's Bible Commentary*, (Grand Rapids: Zondervan, 1976), 173. Cited in Svendsen, 191.

[8]   James G. McCarthy, *The Gospel According to Rome* (Eugene, Oregon: Harvest House, 1995), 188.

[9]   See RCH Lenski, *The Interpretation of St. John's Gospel*, (Minneapolis: Augsburg Publishing House, 1961), 199.

THE PROCLAMATION OF THE KINGDOM OF GOD
(Mark 1:14, 15; 2:3-13)

One of the most significant mysteries of light in the life of Jesus is his proclamation of the Kingdom of God. He made it clear from the very beginning of his ministry on earth that his mission was to help people to understand the Gospel of the Kingdom. He did this by proclaiming the arrival of the Kingdom of God and by demonstrating his divinity and his power.

Proclamation of the Gospel of the Kingdom

St. Mark states:

> After John's had been arrested, Jesus came to Galilee proclaiming the gospel of God. "This is the time of fulfillment. The kingdom of God is at hand! Repent, and believe in the gospel" (1:14, 15).

Description of the Gospel of the Kingdom (v. 14)

The word "*gospel*" means good news. Jesus came to bring good news to humanity. At his birth, the angels proclaimed: "Do not be afraid, for behold, I bring you good news of great joy that will be for all the people. For today in the city of David a savior has been born for you who is Messiah and Lord" Luke 2:10-12). Through out New Testament we find definitions of the various dimensions of the good news that Jesus proclaimed.

Good News of Truth

The gospel is the good news that Jesus came from heaven to earth to share the truth that God loves us and wants us to relate to him as his children. This truth is not an abstract concept; it is personified in Jesus Christ himself. St. John says: "And the Word became flesh and made his dwelling among us, and we saw his glory, the glory as of the Father's only Son, full of grace and truth" (John 1:14). Jesus said: "I am the way, and the truth, and the life. No one comes to the Father except through me" (John 14:6). When Jesus came to earth, many people had erroneous and distorted ideas of the nature and character of God. Through his life and ministry, however, Jesus helped people to understand what God is like. The Gospel is the good news of truth.

Good News of Hope

One of the characteristics of our society is that of pessimism. Human efforts without Christ's guidance and help often lead to despair. Surrounded by a sense of failure and hopelessness, people often feel that it is useless to keep trying to live victorious lives. The apostle Paul expressed this feeling when he said: "For I do not do the good I want, but I do the evil I do not want. So then I discover the principle that when I want to do right, evil is at hand. … Miserable one that I am! Who will deliver me from this mortal body?" (Romans 7:19, 21, 24). But the apostle's quest does not end there. Instead, he points to the solution when he states: "The sting of death is sin, and the power of sin is the law. But thanks be to God who has given us the victory through our Lord Jesus Christ (1 Corinthians 15:56, 57). The Good News of salvation is that we no longer have to depend on our own wisdom and strength to overcome the things that threaten and defeat us. We can depend on Jesus who fills our hearts with hope. "He has now reconciled in his fleshly body through his death, to present you holy, without blemish, and irreproachable before him, provided that you persevere in the faith, firmly grounded, stable, and not shifting from the hope of the gospel that you heard, which has been preached to every creature under heaven, of which I, Paul, am a minister" (Colossians 1:22, 23)

Good News of Peace

On a worldwide scale, the years of genuine peace have been few and far between. Wars, conflict, and strife between nations, socio-cultural groups, and factions mar the peace and tranquility that we all yearn for. On a personal basis, often our spirits appear to be the grounds for civil wars. We experience inner conflict between the good and the bad intentions that compete for dominance in our hearts. Only Jesus can bring genuine peace to our hearts. Jesus said: "Peace I leave with you; my peace I give to you. Not as the world gives do I give it to you. Do not let your hearts be troubled or afraid" (John 14:27). St. Paul affirmed this when he said, "Therefore, since we have been justified by faith, we have peace with God through our Lord Jesus Christ" (Romans 5:1).

Good News of Salvation

The salvation that people receive when they receive Jesus Christ into their hearts has two dimensions. First, it is salvation from penalty of past sin. The Bible says: "The wages of sin is death" (Romans 6:23). Sin separates us from God. It results in God's punishment. Second, salvation has a positive dimension. The second part of the verse just quoted states: "But the gift of God is eternal life in Christ Jesus our Lord." The present dimension of eternal life made possible by Jesus gives us the power to conquer sin and to live victorious lives. The future dimension of eternal life gives the assurance that we will be with Christ in heaven when we die (John 14:1-4).

Invitation to Repentance and Belief (Mark 1:15)

In announcing the Kingdom of God, Jesus called on people to "repent and believe the good news.

Repentance

In Greek the word repentance is *metanoia.* It means *a change of mind.* This involves more than sorrow for the consequences of sin. A person can be very sorry for the situation he has gotten into because of his sin. Down deep, however, he knows that if he could escape the consequences, he would very likely do the same thing again. True repentance requires sorrow for the sin that has been committed. The sin of violating God's laws, missing the mark, of failing to live up to the values established by Christ should bring sorrow to our hearts. We need to remember that it was the sins of humanity (including ours) that made it necessary for Jesus to die on the cross. Repentance, therefore, means genuine sorrow for our sins.

Belief

Jesus did not just call people to repentance; he invited them to place their trust in him (Acts 4:12). Repentance involves turning our backs on our past sins.

Belief involves *acknowledgement,* which means taking and accepting the facts just as they are. Some people think of Jesus only as the baby in the manger or as a dead Christ on the cross. These facts are accurate; however, they are not the complete story. The Bible states that Jesus is the Son of God who took on human form, lived a sinless life, taught divine truths, died on the cross, rose from the dead, is in heaven interceding for us, and is spiritually present in our hearts to help as we go through the experiences of life (Romans 10:9,10: 1 Tim 2:5).

Belief also involves *commitment.* It means that we enter into a personal, spiritual relationship with Jesus Christ. As a couple repeats the wedding vows and says, "I, do," we commit to a personal relationship with Christ when we accept him as our savior and Lord (John 1:12). It is not enough to know about Jesus; we must get to know him personally.

Belief also involves *confidence.* It means full trust, complete reliance, and unwavering certainty that we can stake our very lives and our future on Jesus' word. Because he had put his complete trust in Jesus, the Apostle Paul was able to say: "For I know him in whom I have believed and am confident that he is able to guard what has been entrusted to me until that day" (2 Tim 1:12).

Believing in Jesus, therefore, means accepting what the Bible says about the sacrifice that Jesus offered on the cross to forgive us our sins. When he said on the cross "It is finished," (John 19:30), he completed the work of our salvation. He did everything that was required by God to make our salvation possible. There is, therefore, nothing that we can add to the work of Christ. We must simply repent of our sins and put our trust in Christ. "There is no condemnation for those who are in Christ Jesus" (Romans 8:1).

Let's meditate:

1. By studying the teachings of Jesus we have learned that the Gospel is the Good News of hope and peace. Do we have hope and peace in our hearts today?

2. Can we truthfully say with the songwriter: "It is well with my soul"?

3. Believing in Jesus involves acknowledgement, commitment, and confidence.

4. Have we acknowledged the basic truths about the life and ministry of Jesus?

5. Have we made a commitment to receive him in our hearts and follow him the rest of our lives?

6. Do we have the confidence that if we have put our trust in him as our only Savior, we will be with him in heaven when we die?

Demonstration of the Power and Divinity of the Proclaimer (2:1-13)

The Situation (vv. 1-5)

When Jesus arrived in Capernaum, a large crowd gathered in his home to hear his teachings. While he was speaking, four men arrived carrying a paralyzed man. Because the house was completely full, these men decided to carve out a hole in the roof and lower the paralyzed man in a stretcher (v. 4).

Jesus was touched by "their faith" (the men's and the paralytic's) that he decided to grant their petition (v. 4). Jesus, however, did not heal the man immediately. Instead, he made the statement "Child, your sins are forgiven" (v. 5). Jewish people, including their religious leaders, believed that the reason why people were sick was that they had sinned. It could well be that the paralytic himself held this belief and felt castigated by God as well as alienated from him. At the very outset, Jesus reassures this man by calling him "child." In so doing, he was conveying the thought "Cheer up, God is not angry with you. Every thing is going to be all right." Jesus conveyed to him that God was not like the religious leaders had portrayed him: stern, severe, austere, judgmental and aloof. The God that Jesus came to reveal through his words and actions has a loving and forgiving heart. These words must have sounded as music to the paralytic's ears. He said: "your sins are forgiven." The literal translation is "your sins are dismissed." The Bible speaks clearly about God's willingness to forgive and forget our sins once we have repented and asked him for forgiveness. The Bible uses several analogies to nail down this point. Our sins are "cast to the depths of the sea" (Micah 7:19). They are removed from the record, wiped out, remembered no more (Isaiah 43:25). Our sins are removed as far as the east from the west (Psalm 103:12). When our repentance is genuine, God's forgiveness is complete. The statement by Jesus "your sins are dismissed," immediately caught the attention of the Jewish religious leaders.

The Argument (vv. 6-7)

The religious leaders immediately questioned Jesus' authority to make this type of a statement. They were correct in asserting, "God alone can forgive sins" (v. 7). The Bible makes it clear that only God has the authority to forgive sins. All of us as human beings are sinners (Romans 3:23). God alone is sinless and is the only one who can forgive us of our sins. The religious leaders were right in making this statement.

Where the religious leaders were wrong was that they did not acknowledge that Jesus is God. He is God the Son, the second person of the Holy Trinity. Because they did not know who Jesus really was, they accused him of blasphemy. In essence, they were saying: "Jesus is insulting God by pretending to take his place." The penalty for blasphemy at that time was death by stoning. The religious leaders felt that at last, they had caught Jesus sinning against God and this would give them the justification to put him to death.

Jesus, being God the Son, read the thoughts and discerned the spirits of the religious leaders. He startled them by saying: "Why are you thinking such things in your hearts? Which is easier, to say to the paralytic, your sins are forgiven, or to say, Rise, pick up your mat and walk?" (vv. 8, 9).

The Miracle (vv. 9-12)

Obviously, the statement "your sins are forgiven" would have been easier to make because it did not require any external verification. Anyone could have made that statement and no one would have had any tangible proof that the forgiveness of sins had taken place. Jesus, however, provided proof of his divine origin by performing a miracle.

"But that you may know that the Son of Man has authority to forgive sins on earth"- he said this to the paralytic, "I say to you, rise, pick up your mat, and go home." "He rose, picked up his mat at once, and went away in the sight of everyone" (Vv. 11, 12).

It was clear that Jesus had performed a miracle. Everyone saw the paralytic brought in by the four men. They heard the words of Jesus. Then they saw the man not only healed, but also empowered immediately to walk and to carry his mat with him. The reason that he performed this miracle was "That you may know that the Son of Man has authority to forgive sins."

The Response

The Bible makes it clear that many of the people who saw this miracle believed in Jesus. The proof is that they "glorified God, saying, "We have never seen anything like this" (v. 12). There is no evidence, however, that the Pharisees believed that Jesus was the Son of God after seeing this miracle. In the very next chapter we see evidence that they continued to question Jesus' authority.

Let us meditate:

1. Jesus revealed God as a loving and forgiving Father. What image do we have of God?

2. Jesus told the paralyzed man that his sins are "forgiven." Do we have the assurance that our sins have been forgiven and forgotten by God?

3. When the people saw the miracle that Jesus performed, they believed in Jesus and praised God. After seeing evidence of the divine nature of Jesus in the Bible as well as in our lives, have we believed in him as our personal and all-sufficient savior?

Bible Memory Verse:

"Child, your sins are forgiven" (Mark 2:5).

Prayer:

Dear Jesus, like the paralyzed man and his companions, I want to put my faith in you. Deliver me from the things that paralyze me and keep me from walking victoriously in your presence, Amen.

83

THE TRANSFIGURATION OF JESUS
(Luke 9:28-36)

John Paul II has called the transfiguration of Jesus "the Mystery of light par excellance."[1] In this experience, the "glory of the Godhead shines forth from the face of Jesus."[2] This event is not only witnessed by the inner circle of disciples of Jesus (Peter, John, and James), but is confirmed by two patriarchs representing the Covenant of God with his people. Jesus, the patriarchs, and the disciples, are engulfed in a cloud, which provides visible evidence of God's glory. These divine manifestations were brought about by God for a very special purpose that related directly to the divine nature of Jesus and the temporal and eternal dimensions of his mission on earth.

The Prayer Meeting (v. 28)

"About eight days after he said this, he took Peter, John and James and went up the mountain to pray." Jesus had said: "There are some standing here who will not taste death until they see the kingdom of God" (v. 27). While some later thought that Jesus was referring to his Second Coming to earth, this was a reference to the manifestation of God's glory in the Transfiguration of Jesus. It is obvious that the three disciples that Jesus invited to join him in prayer at the mountain were not aware of the marvelous experience that awaited them. They simply accepted his invitation pray.

Throughout his earthly ministry Jesus took time to get away from the pressures of the crowds and spend time alone with God. His prayer in the Garden of Gethsemane is an example of the way in which Jesus sought the will of the Father (Mark 14:32-42). The prayer of Jesus recorded in John 17 reveals the petitions that he presented to the Father on behalf of his followers. Jesus' prayer in Matthew 11:25-27, reveals his intimate knowledge about and his intimate relationship with the heavenly Father. The prayer now known as "The Lord's Prayer," was shared by Jesus with his disciples when they asked him "Lord, teach us to pray." They had observed the prayer disciplines of Jesus and their effect upon him and upon others. This motivated them to request help from the Lord regarding their prayer lives. Through prayer, Jesus stayed in touch with his heavenly Father, sought his will, and interceded for his disciples. It was not unusual therefore, that Jesus would invite these three disciples to spend time in prayer with him in a secluded place.

The Manifestation (v. 29)

"While he was praying his face changed in appearance and his clothes became dazzlingly white."

This implies an internal as well as an external source of illumination. The face of Jesus changed in appearance. There was a glow that came from within. The fullness of the Spirit illuminated his entire being. This was indicative of the fact that the fullness of the Godhead dwelt within him. At the appointed time, these three disciples were given the opportunity to see the overwhelming evidence of the divinity of Jesus. There was the brilliancy from within as well as the glow of God' glory resulting in the external radiance of Jesus' garments.

This was the actual manifestation of God's presence in and around Jesus. It distinguished Jesus from any other human being that ever walked the face of this earth. Jesus is the only human/divine being who ever existed. Because of this John was able to write: "And the Word became flesh and made his dwelling among us, and we saw his glory, the glory as of the Father's only Son, full of grace and truth" (John 1:14).

The Heavenly Visitors (vv. 30-33)

The Significance of Their Appearance

"And behold, two men were conversing with him, Moses and Elijah who appeared in glory and spoke of his exodus that he was going to accomplish in Jerusalem" (v. 30).

Moses and Elijah, as representatives of the Ancient Covenant that God had made with his people, came from heaven to earth to consecrate Jesus who would die on the Cross, not long after this event. The presence of Moses, the supreme Lawgiver, and Elijah, the first and greatest of the Prophets brought affirmation to Jesus as he made preparation for his sacrificial death. Barclay states:

It meant that they saw in Jesus the consummation of all they had dreamed of in the past. It meant that they saw in Him all that history had longed and hoped for and looked forward to. It is as if at that moment Jesus was assured that He was on the right way because all history had been leading up to the Cross.[3]

It must have been comforting for Jesus to speak with the two glorified patriarchs who understood what he was going to go through on the Cross. Several times he had attempted to share with his disciples what was in store for him at Calvary but they simply did not understand. No mere human being could understand the physical and spiritual agony that Jesus would experience as he bore on his body and soul the sins of the world. The Bible says, "For our sake he made him to be sin who did not know sin, so that we might become the righteousness of God in him" (2 Corinthians 5:21).

The disciples had been shattered by Jesus' announcement that he had to go to Jerusalem and be put to death (Mark 8:31). For them it was incredible and incomprehensible that the Messiah would have to give up his life on a cruel Cross. They saw the Messiah as an irresistible conqueror, not as a sacrificial offering. Witnessing the transfiguration would give these disciples something to hold on to. They did not fully understand the divine/human mission of Jesus. This would not happen until after the resurrection of Jesus. When they did understand this, they were willing to stake their very lives on the divine truths that had been revealed to them. Peter later wrote: "We did not follow cleverly devised myths when we made known to you the power and coming of our Lord Jesus Christ, but we had been eyewitnesses of his majesty. For he received honor and glory from God the Father when that unique declaration came to him from the majestic glory, 'This is my Son, my beloved, with whom I am well pleased.' We ourselves heard this voice come from heaven while we were with him on the holy mountain" (2 Peter 1:16,17). John also wrote, "We saw his glory, the glory as of the Father's only Son, full of grace and truth" (John 1:14). The transfiguration branded like a hot iron on the hearts of these disciples the fact that Jesus Christ is the Son of God and there is no one else like him in the entire universe.

Let's Meditate:

1. In light of the transfiguration, what position does Jesus Christ occupy in our hearts and minds?

2. Is Jesus just one of many religious leaders described in the Bible or Does he occupy a unique place in our hearts?

3. Is he just a Prophet as the Samaritan woman first thought (John 4:19) or the Messiah as she later found out (John 4:25)?

The Response of the Earthly Witnesses (v. 33)

> "As they were about to part from him, Peter said to Jesus, "Master, it is good that we are here; let us make three tents, one for you, one for Moses, and one for Elijah." But he did not know what he was saying."

When Peter, John, and James saw the glory of God in and around Jesus and they saw Moses and Elijah talking with him, they were totally amazed. Peter verbalized their feelings when he said, "Master, it is good that we are here." It was such an indescribable feeling of felicity that he is almost child-like in expressing himself. He was so overcome by this experience that he didn't quite know how to put his feelings into sensible words. There is also the thought that he wanted this experience to last forever. The three tents were to be for Jesus and the two heavenly witnesses. He did not even think about himself and his fellow disciples. He simply wanted to hold on to the heavenly presence before it vanished from his eyes. The presence of the glorified Savior brings indescribable joy to those who receive him in their hearts.

Let's Meditate:

1. Do we believe it is possible to experience the presence of Jesus in our lives?

2. Are we content simply to know *about* Jesus instead of *knowing him* in a personal way?

3. Does our spiritual experience consist merely of observing a set of rules or following religious practices?

4. Can we experience the living presence of Christ in our hearts as we read the Bible and talk to him directly as we pray?

The Cloud (v. 34)

"While he was still speaking, a cloud came and cast a shadow over them, and they became frightened when they entered the cloud."

Based on their history Jewish persons associated the presence of God with the cloud. It was a cloud that surrounded Moses when he met God. As the people of God traveled through the wilderness, the Shekinah was symbol of the glory of God. This cloud, which hovered over the Tabernacle, gave the Hebrew pilgrims the assurance that God was with them. When the cloud moved, that was the signal for them to travel onward (Exodus 40:34-38). At the transfiguration of Jesus, the Shekinah glory of God covered Jesus and those who were with him. The cloud that had formerly filled the sanctuary of the Lord, now receives Jesus and his companions into the tabernacle of glory. This provided for the disciples a powerful confirmation of the divinity of Christ and of his earthly mission.

The Voice (v. 35)

Then from the cloud came a voice that said:

"This is my chosen Son; listen to him."

The same voice that had spoken at the baptism of Jesus (Luke 3:22, Matthew 3:17) and at the Temple (John 12:28), spoke again to confirm God's unique relationship with Jesus. It also provided an affirmation of Jesus' ministry. This underscores the uniqueness of Jesus in the entire universe. He is the only one God described as "his Son." Jesus referred to this unique relationship when he said to Nicodemus: "For God so loved the world that he gave his only Son, so that everyone who believes in him might not perish but might have eternal life" (John 3:16).

"Listen to him." Despite the distinguished history and powerful ministries of Moses and Elijah, God does not say listen to them. They, like John the Baptizer, were precursors, but Jesus is the "Chosen One," the Savior of the World.

Let's meditate:

1. To whom do we listen when we have serious questions or encounter difficult decisions in our lives?

2. Is there any significance to the fact that God did not instruct the disciples to listen to Moses and Elijah?

3. Can we listen to Jesus when we study his teachings in the Bible?

4. Who is our ultimate authority when we have questions about our eternal destiny, Jesus or someone else?

The Central Figure (v. 36)

"After the voice had spoken, Jesus was found alone.
They fell silent and did not at that time tell anyone what
they had seen."

Moses and Elijah had very significant missions here on earth. When they came to the end of their journey, God took them to heaven. At the transfiguration God brought them to earth to consecrate the Messiah for his sacrificial death. The role of Moses and Elijah was limited to bearing witnesses to the divine nature of Jesus. Jesus did not pray to them. He did not ask Moses and Elijah to intercede for the disciples. He did not instruct the disciples to pray to Moses and Elijah. They had their place in God's plan for his people. When they completed their mission, however, they left. Jesus alone remained. Jesus, therefore, is the only Savior of the world. Many people have served God through their lives, yet they did not die on the Cross for our sins. Peter and John, witnesses of the transfiguration, urged people to put their faith in Jesus as their only Savior.

St. Peter said:

"He is 'the stone rejected by you, the builders, which
has become the cornerstone.' There is no salvation through
anyone else, nor is there any other name under heaven given

to the human race by which we are to be saved" (Acts 4:11,12)

St. John stated:

"Now Jesus did many other signs in the presence of [his] disciples that are not written in this book. But these are written that you may [come to] believe that Jesus is the Messiah, the Son of God, and that through this belief you may have life in his name" (John 20:30,31).

The Bible says:

"Therefore, since we have a great high priest who has passed through the heavens, Jesus, the Son of God, let us hold fast to our confession. For we do not have a high priest who is unable to sympathize with our weaknesses, but one who has similarly been tested in every way, yet without sin. So let us confidently approach the throne of grace to receive mercy and to find grace for timely help." (Hebrews 4:14,15)

Jesus himself said:

"I am the way and the truth and the life. No one comes to the Father except through me" (John 14:6).

Let's Meditate:

1. Who is the only one who can give us our eternal salvation?

2. To whom should we direct our prayers?

3. In light of the teachings in this portion of the Bible, can we conclude that we can have appreciation and respect for other persons, who served God, yet we should pray directly to Jesus?

4. Who is the only one who can save us from our sins?

5. How should we approach the throne of grace as we pray, with fear or confidence?

Bible Memory Verse:

"This is my chosen Son; listen to Him" (Luke 9:35).

Prayer:

Heavenly Father, I thank you for sending your Son, Jesus Christ to die on the cross for my sins. I repent of my sins and invite your Son to become my Savior and Lord. Thank you for hearing my prayer, Amen.

End Notes

1   John Paul II, *Apostolic Letter*, 11. http://www.vatican.va/holy_father/john_paul_ii/ apost_letters/documents/hf_jp-ii_apl_20021016_rosarium-virginis-mariae_en.html

2   Ibid.

3   William Barclay, *The Gospel of Mark*, (Philadelphia: Westminster Press, 1956), 216.

THE INSTITUTION OF THE EUCHARIST
(Luke 22:7-20)

The Eucharist has had profound significance for Christians throughout the centuries. It is at the very heart of Jesus' saving mission on this earth. John Paul II refers to this mystery as the one in which Jesus, "testifies 'to the end' his love for humanity (John 13:1), for whose salvation he will offer himself in sacrifice."[1] When Jesus instituted the Eucharist, he taught his disciples the meaning of the sacrificial death on the cross that he was about to experience. Knowing that his disciples were aware of the historical and religious implications of the Passover, Jesus utilized that occasion to instruct them about the infinitely greater deliverance they would receive as a result of his death on the cross. Today, we can view the Eucharist in terms of its past, its present, and its future perspectives. Viewing the Eucharist from the perspective of the past motivates us to focus on its original institution by Jesus Christ. Viewing the Eucharist from the perspective of the present motivates us to seek to discover what it means for us to participate in it properly and worthily in our day and time. Viewing it from the perspective of the future inspires us to know that the time will come when all of us who have put our faith and trust in Jesus as our Savior and Lord will celebrate the Eucharist in heaven with him (Luke 22:18).

Let us look at the preparation for the Eucharist, the institution of the Eucharist, and the implications of the Eucharist.

The Preparation for the Eucharist (vv. 7-13)

Jesus instituted the Eucharist in connection with the celebration of the Passover. The Passover feast commemorated the liberation of the Jewish people from their bondage in Egypt. It had rich historical, spiritual, and symbolic meaning, which pointed to the coming of the Messiah. In his divine wisdom, Jesus chose this occasion to institute the Eucharist, thus making a connection between the sacrifice of the Passover lamb and the infinitely greater sacrifice that he, the Lamb of God (John 1:29), would offer for the sins of the world.

CHAPTER 10

The Customary Preparation

In accordance with Jewish custom, preparation for the celebration of the Passover was very precise and deliberate. There were certain things that needed to be done in order for the celebration to be considered appropriate historically and spiritually.[2]

The Search for the Leaven

The first step in the preparation for the Passover was to search for leaven. Prior to the celebration every particle of leaven needed to be removed from the house. This pointed back to the unleavened bread that the Jewish people ate at the first Passover as they were escaping from Egypt. Unleavened bread could be baked more quickly than leavened bread, which would require time for the leaven to rise. In addition to commemorating the haste in which they had left Egypt, eating unleavened bread conveyed the meaning of purity. Leaven, was seen by the Jewish people as a symbol of corruption. It was identified with fermentation and putrefaction. The day before the Passover, it was customary for the head of the household to take a lighted candle and search for leaven.

The Sacrifice of the Passover Lamb

The sacrifice of the Passover Lamb took place on the afternoon before Passover evening. Everyone went to the Temple. The worshipper was required to slay his own lamb, thus making his own sacrifice. As he slit the lamb's throat, the priests would place the blood in a bowl and dash it upon the altar. In Jewish thought, blood was associated with life. The life of the lamb, therefore, was being sacrificed for the sins of the worshiper. The lamb was then carried home, roasted on an open fire, and eaten as the Passover meal.

The Passover Meal

The Passover Meal had several items that were rich in historical value and symbolism.

The Lamb

The lamb reminded the Jewish people of the lamb that each family had slain in Egypt and the blood they had sprinkled on the lintels and the doorposts of their houses. These were the houses that the Angel of the Lord spared as he slew every first-born in the land of Egypt (Exodus 12:21-29). This was the punishment it took for Pharaoh to grant permission for the Jewish people to leave Egypt (Exodus 12:30-32). The sacrifice of the lamb, therefore, had great significance for the Jewish people, especially during the celebration of the Passover when their houses were passed over by the Angel of the Lord.

The Unleavened Bread

In the celebration of the meal, the Jewish people did not just get rid of the leavened bread; they baked unleavened bread. This reminded them of the haste in which they had left Egypt (Exodus 12:14,15).

The Bowl of Salt Water

At every celebration of the Passover, there was a bowl, which contained salt water. This reminded the Jewish people of the waters of the Red Sea that they miraculously crossed when the Egyptian army was pursuing them (Exodus 14:10-30).

The Paste

At the Passover meal there was also a paste called *Carosheth,* which was a mixture of dates, pomegranates, apples, and nuts. This reminded them of the clay their ancestors had used to make bricks when they served as slaves in Egypt. They put sticks of cinnamon through the clay to remind them of the straw they had used in the bricks that they made.

The Cups of Wine

At the Passover celebration, there were also four cups of wine that were drunk at different stages of the meal. This reminded them of the four promises that God had made to them in Exodus 6:7-7. For them, these promises were a covenant, an agreement that God had made with them as his people. These promises, found in Exodus 6:6,7, were:

> "I will free you from the forced labor of the Egyptians."
> "I will deliver you from their slavery."
> "I will rescue you by my outstretched arm and with mighty acts of judgment."
> "I will take you as my own people, and you shall have me as your God."

95

In light of the fact that every detail of the Passover meal had profound historical and symbolic significance, preparation for this celebration was of utmost importance. It commemorated the day when God had delivered the Jewish people from their bondage in Egypt. There were numerous aspects of this meal, which pointed to the liberation from sin that people would experience as a result of the sacrifice of the Lamb of God on the Cross of Calvary.

The Preparation Jesus Made

When the day of the Feast of Unleavened Bread arrived, the day for sacrificing the Passover lamb, Jesus sent out Peter and John, instructing them, "Go and make preparations for us to eat the Passover." They asked him, "Where do you want us to make the preparations?" And he answered them, "When you go into the city, a man will meet you carrying a jar of water. Follow him into the house that he enters and say to the master of the house, 'The teacher says to you, Where is the guest room where I may eat the Passover with my disciples?' He will show you a large upper room that is furnished. Make the preparations there." Then they went off and found everything exactly as he had told them, and there they prepared the Passover."'(Vv. 7-13).

This passage of Scripture makes it very clear that Jesus considered this event so important and special that he made arrangements in advance so that everything would be in its proper place during the celebration of this memorial feast known as the Passover. He wanted the supper to be prepared in advance. He also wanted the place in which it was celebrated to be appropriate for the occasion. Verse 13 affirms the fact that "they went off and found everything exactly as he had told them" and that the Passover supper was prepared in accordance with the instructions Jesus had given them. Jesus was undoubtedly concerned with the details of the celebration of the Passover. Every detail was important because of its historical and symbolic implications. Even more important than this for Jesus was the fact that he wanted to spend an evening of undisturbed fellowship and prayer with his disciples.

The Celebration of the Passover

"When the hour had arrived, he took his place at the table, and the apostles with him. He said to them: 'I have eagerly desired to eat this Passover this Passover with you before I suffer, for, I tell you, I shall not eat it again until there is fulfillment in the kingdom of God'" (vv. 14-16).

It is absolutely remarkable that Jesus is at this time fully aware of his impending death on the Cross. He makes this very clear when he expresses his desire to celebrate the Passover before he suffers. He is not, however, thinking about himself or even about Judas who was about to betray him. Instead Jesus focuses upon his disciples for whom he is not only their Redeemer but also their friend.[3] He has especially longed for this reunion because he loved his disciples dearly and wanted to spend this time of rich fellowship with them. There is a sense in which this was a farewell feast for him. He would not have a feast like this with them "until it is fulfilled in the Kingdom of God." This feast would prepare his disciples for the institution of the Lord's Supper, the Eucharist that would for the centuries to come commemorate his sacrificial death. The Passover celebration prepared the way for the institution of the Eucharist. Jesus, however, points beyond the earthly celebration of the Eucharist. "The Lord points to the eternal coronation feast of His glorified Church, the shinning image of the eternal supper, the anticipatory celebration of which the New Testament covenant meal He is now to establish. As our Savior in the paschal lamb sees the type of His own immaculate sacrifice, so does He see in the paschal celebration a symbolic setting forth of the perfect joy in heaven."[4] For the disciples as well as for the Church, the Eucharist had not only a present dimension, but an eternal one as well. This is what makes the Eucharist such a significant observance for us today.

The Institution of the Eucharist

The celebration of the Passover followed very specific steps: 1) the Cup of the Kiddush (sanctification) which the head of the family took, prayed over it and then all drank of it; 2) the first hand washing; 3) the eating of the parsley or lettuce; 4) the breaking of the bread; 5) the relating of the story of Deliverance; 6) the singing of Psalms 113 and 114; 7) the drinking of the second cup (of Proclaiming); 8) the second washing of hands; 9) the saying of grace; 10) the eating of bitter herbs; 11) the meal proper; 12) the third washing of hands; 13) the remainder of the unleavened bread eaten; 14) the prayer of thanksgiving and the third cup is drunk; 15) the second part of the *Hallel* (Psalms 115-118) is sung; 16) the fourth cup is drunk and Psalm 136 is sung; and 16) two short prayers are said.[5] The writers of the Gospels do not give specific information regarding the celebration of the Passover other than to state that they did celebrate it. The institution of the Eucharist was a special act in the course of the Passover celebration. Jesus allied the Eucharist with the ancient feast of his people so that it would be dramatically imprinted in the minds of his followers. At the appropriate moment in the celebration, Jesus took two items from the Passover meal which were rich in historic and symbolic value and gave them new and eternal meaning as he instituted the Eucharist. These were the Cup and the Bread.

The Cup

> Then he took a cup, gave thanks, and said, "Take this and share it among yourselves; for I tell you that from this time on I shall not drink of the fruit of the vine until the kingdom of God comes." "This cup is the new covenant in my blood, which will be shed for you" (Luke 22:17,18,20).

At the Passover meal, the head of the family took the cup and prayed over it, and then all drank of it.[6] The customary prayer at the celebration of the Passover was: "Blessed be thou, O Lord our God, the King of the world, who hast created the fruit of the vine."[7] After offering a prayer, Jesus passed the cup so that his disciples could partake of it.

The partaking of the cup took on a new meaning when Jesus said: "This is the new covenant in my blood." The old covenant, which God had established with his people, was sealed with the blood of the animals that had been offered as a sacrifice unto God. Exodus 24 reads:

> When Moses came to the people and related all the words and ordinances of the Lord, they all answered with one voice, "We will do everything that the Lord has told us." Moses then wrote down all the words of the Lord and, rising early the next day, he erected at the foot of the mountain an altar and twelve pillars for the twelve tribes of Israel. Then having certain young men of the Israelites to offer holocausts and sacrifice young bulls as peace offerings to the Lord, Moses took half of the blood and put it in large bowls; the other half he splashed on the altar. Taking the book of the covenant, he read it aloud to the people, who answered, 'All that the Lord has said, we will heed and do.' Then he took the blood and sprinkled it on the people saying, 'This is the blood of the covenant which the Lord has made with you in accordance with all these words of his.' (Vv. 3-8)

At the institution of the Eucharist, Jesus established a new covenant (agreement) with the people who would put their trust in him. This new covenant is described in the book of Hebrews:

This is the covenant I will establish with them after
those days, says the Lord: "I will put my laws in their hearts,
and I will write them upon their minds." He also says, "Their
sins and evildoing I will remember no more. Where there
is forgiveness of these, there is no longer offering for sin"
(Hebrews 10:16-18).

This new covenant was fulfilled in Jesus, through his sacrifice on the
cross. The old covenant was sealed with the blood of the animals that were
offered in sacrifice. The new covenant was sealed with the precious blood of
Jesus. He said: "This cup is the new covenant in my blood, which will be
shed for you." Based on the confidence of the perfect sacrifice that Jesus
offered for us on the Cross, St. John was able to affirm: "But if we walk in
the light as he is in the light, then we have fellowship with one another, and
the blood of his Son Jesus cleanses us from all sin" (1 John 1:7). The writer
of the book of Hebrews explains: "He has no need, as did the high priests, to
offer sacrifice day after day, first for his own sins and then for those of the
people; he did that once for all when he offered himself" (Hebrews 7:27). He
adds: "By this 'will' we have been consecrated through the offering of the
body of Jesus Christ once for all. Every priest stands daily, at his ministry,
offering frequently those same sacrifices that can never take away sins. But
this one [Jesus] offered one sacrifice for sins, and took his seat forever at the
right hand of God" (Hebrews 10:10-12).

The Bread

"Then he took the bread, said the blessing, broke it,
and gave it to them, saying, This is my body, which will be
given for you; do this in memory of me" (v. 19).

During the Passover meal, two blessings were used at the breaking of
bread. "Blessed be You, O Lord, our God, King of the Universe, who brings
forth fruit from the earth." Or, "Blessed are You, our Father in heaven who
gives us today the bread necessary for us."[8] The unleavened bread reminded
the Jews of the bread of affliction that they ate in Egypt. It was broken to
remind them that slaves never had a whole loaf, but only broken crusts to eat.
The head of the family would say: "This is the bread of affliction which our
forefathers ate in the land of Egypt. Whosoever is hungry let him come and
eat. Whosoever is in need let him come and keep the Passover with us."[9]

CHAPTER 10

When Jesus broke the bread at the institution of the Eucharist, he kept the idea of brokenness, but he applied it to the brokenness that his body would undergo as a result of his sacrifice on the cross. Isaiah, the Prophet, had prophesied that the body of Jesus would be broken:

> Who would believe what we have heard? To whom has the arm of the Lord been revealed? He grew up like a sapling before him, like a shoot from the parched earth. There was in him no stately bearing to make us look at him, nor the appearance that would attract us to him. He was spurned and avoided by men, a man of suffering, accustomed to infirmity, one of those from whom men hide their faces, spurned, and we held him in no esteem. Yet it was our infirmities that he bore, our sufferings that he endured, while we thought of him as stricken, as one smitten by God and afflicted. But he was pierced for our offenses, crushed for our sins, upon him was the chastisement that makes us whole, by his stripes we were healed. We had all gone astray like sheep, but God laid upon him the guilt of us all" (Isaiah 53:1-6).

This is exactly what Jesus experienced in his body when he offered himself as God's sacrifice on the cruel cross. He was beaten, a crown of thorns was put on his head, nails pierced his hands and his feet, and a spear pierced his side. The body of Jesus was broken on our behalf. John, the Baptist had said of him: "Behold, the Lamb of God, who takes away the sins of the world!" (John 1:29) Just as a lamb was slain to bear the sins of the sinner, Jesus offered his body to be slain for our sins. The sacrifices of the lambs had to be offered over and over again. The sacrifice of Jesus on the cross for our sins was offered once and for all. "For by one offering he has made perfect forever those who are being consecrated" (Hebrews 10:14). We cannot do anything to merit our salvation; what we need to do is accept Jesus as the only one who can save us, because he is the only one who died for us on the Cross.

Let's Meditate:

As Jesus instituted the Eucharist, he said: "Do this in memory of me" (v. 19).

1. When we partake of the wine, do we meditate on the blood of Jesus that was shed for us on the cross?

2. When we partake of the bread, do we meditate on the body of Jesus that was broken on our behalf?

3. When we partake of the Eucharist do we think about the purpose Jesus had for dying on the Cross?

4. Have we accepted the sacrifice of Jesus on the cross as the perfect sacrifice for our sins, or are we trying to save ourselves through our own efforts?

5. Have we received Jesus as our only savior?

Bible Memory Verse:

"But this one [Jesus] offered one sacrifice for sins, and took his seat forever at the right hand of God" (Hebrews 10:12).

Prayer:

Dear Jesus, I thank you from the bottom of my heart for offering your blood and your body as a sacrifice for me. I receive you as my only savior Forgive me of my sins and come to live in my heart. Amen

End Notes

[1] John Paul II, *Apostolic Letter, op., cit., 11*.

[2] William Barclay, *The Gospel of Mark,*(Philadelphia: Westminster Press, 1956), 347-350.

[3] Lange, *The Gospel According to Luke*, 336.

[4] Ibid.,336.

[5] William Barclay, op. cit., 353-56.

[6] Ibid., 353.

[7] Lange, *The Gospel According to Luke*, 336.

[8] William Barclay, op. cit., 355.

[9]   Ibid., 354.

PART THREE:

THE SORROWFUL MYSTERIES

The Sorrowful Mysteries are given great prominence in the Bible. All of the writers of the Gospels dedicate significant portions to the events that marked this phase in the earthly ministry of Jesus. These events are recorded by the evangelists so that individuals may find the revelation of God's love and the source of salvation.

The sequence of these mysteries begins with *The Agony of Jesus in the Garden*. There at Gethsemane Jesus prayed the most crucial prayer of his earthly ministry: "Father, if you are willing, take this cup away from me; still not my will but yours be done" (Luke 22:42). This was followed by *The Scourging at the Pillar* (Matthew 27:25-26). The people chose Barabbas to be freed instead of Jesus. Before turning him over to be crucified, Pilate allowed the soldiers to scourge Jesus. *The Crowning with Thorns* (Matthew 27:28-29) was then done by the soldiers who were mocking Jesus. This was followed by *The Carrying of the Cross* (John 19:17-18). The beating Jesus had received had been so brutal that he collapsed as he carried the cross. The soldiers then ordered Simon of Cyrene to carry the cross. This culminated in *The Crucifixion and Death* of Jesus (Luke 23:45-46).

The *Sorrowful Mysteries* help us to understand the extent of Christ's suffering and the depth of his love for us. He loved us so much that he humbled himself "becoming obedient to death, even death on a cross" (Philippians 2:8). May our meditation on the *Sorrowful Mysteries* open our hearts to receive the one who died on the Cross for our salvation.

THE AGONY IN THE GARDEN OF GETHSEMANE
(Luke 22:39-46)

The series of *Sorrowful Mysteries* begins with *The Agony in the Garden of Gethsemane*. On several occasions Jesus had told his disciples that he was going to go to Jerusalem and give up his life for the salvation of humanity. Finally, the time had come for all of the prophecies about his death on the cross to be fulfilled (Luke 22:22). "Then going out he went, as was his custom, to the Mount of Olives, and the disciples followed him" (Luke 22:39).

Jesus' Yearning for Human Fellowship

As he approached the hour of his death, Jesus felt a strong desire for human fellowship. His desire to have human fellowship pointed to the fact that Jesus was truly human. As St. John put it, "and the Word became flesh and made his dwelling among us" (John 1:14). We can understand Jesus' desire for human fellowship. When we face difficulties, we want someone to be with us. Often what is important to us is not so much the words that they say but the fact that they are with us. We simply do not want to be alone when we lose loved ones, or when we are facing our own struggle to overcome illness and sorrow. Someone has said that having loved ones around us multiplies our joys when we are happy and divides our sorrows when we are sad. Jesus sincerely yearned for the presence of his disciples as the hour of his death approached. He said to them: "My soul is sorrowful even to death. Remain here and keep watch" (Mark 14:34).

It is sad, however, to point out those who had affirmed that they were willing to give up their lives for Jesus (Mark 14:31), fell asleep while Jesus was agonizing in the Garden. There was undoubtedly a tone of disappointment and hurt in his voice when he asked them, "Why are you sleeping" (Luke 22:46). The humanity of Jesus is seen clearly in this passage of Scripture. Physically, he is already anticipating the excruciating pain that he is going to experience on the cross. Emotionally, he was feeling the pang of loneliness because his disciples did not understand the meaning of the sacrifice he was about to offer. Following the Lord's Supper, shortly after Judas had left, the disciples had gotten into an argument as to who would be the greatest (Luke

22:24). Then at Gethsemane, they went to sleep while Jesus was praying. Jesus was truly a "man of sorrows," one who was "acquainted with our grief" (Isaiah 53:3). That is the reason why Jesus understands us more than anyone else. The Bible says: "Therefore, since we have a great high priest who has passed through the heavens, Jesus, the Son of God, let us hold fast to our confession. For we do not have a high priest who is unable to sympathize with our weaknesses, but one who has similarly been tested in every way, yet without sin. So let us confidently approach the throne of grace to receive mercy and to find grace for timely help" (Hebrews 4:14-16).

Let's Meditate:

1. Are we fully aware of the awesome physical, emotional, and spiritual price Jesus paid on the Cross, as he died for our sins?

2. Do we truly believe that Jesus can sympathize with us in our loneliness, weaknesses, struggles and failures?

3. Are we at the point when we can approach Jesus confidently with our prayers and petitions?

Jesus' Yearning for Divine Fellowship

"He advanced a little and fell to the ground, praying that if it were possible this hour might pass by him" (Mark 14:35).

Jesus Did Not Want To Die

From a human standpoint, Jesus was not excited about the thought of dying. He was a young man in the prime of his life. There were many things that he still felt he could accomplish. There were many persons that he felt responsible for. There were many friends that he treasured and he wanted to continue to fellowship with them. Aside from this, Jesus knew what a crucifixion was like. He undoubtedly was aware that at times penitents stayed on the cross for as long as a week, slowly bleeding, asphyxiating, and starving to death. He shuddered at the thought of dying such a cruel death. So profound was the agony of Jesus that Luke explains that "his sweat became like drops of blood falling on the ground" (Luke 22:44). The struggle he was going through was so intense that the sweat of Jesus was mixed with blood. The agony was so deep that the small veins near the skin burst and permitted the blood go out with the sweat. It was like the sweat that fell to the ground. "The Cross would lose all its value if it had been easy for Jesus. He had to compel himself to go on."[1]

Jesus Wanted to Know If
There was Some Other Way

"He said, 'Abba, Father, all things are possible to you.
Take this cup away from me" (Mark 14:36).

In saying, "You have the power to do all things," Jesus was acknowledging God's awesome power, even to bring about the salvation of humanity without Jesus having to die that cruel death. It is true that God is all-powerful, but it is also true that God is a holy and just God. As such, he could not let the sins of the world go unpunished. Neither could he allow people in all their sinfulness to draw near to him. The sacrifice of Jesus on the cross was necessary to pay for our sins and make us acceptable to God. The Bible says: "Without the shedding of blood, there is no forgiveness" (Hebrews 9:22). St. Peter affirmed this when he said: "Realizing that you were ransomed from your futile conduct, handed on by your ancestors, not with perishable things like silver or gold but with the precious blood of Christ as of a spotless unblemished lamb" (1 Peter 1:18-20). St. John also affirmed this fact when he said: "The blood of his Son Jesus cleanses us from all sin" (1 John 1:7).

While agonizing at the Garden of Gethsemane, Jesus kept asking his heavenly Father: "Take this cup away from me." God, with a broken heart, did not grant his Son this request. Because of his love for us God did not spare his own son but handed him over for the sake of all of us. Jesus himself explained it this way: "For God so loved the world that he gave his only Son, so that everyone who believes in him might not perish but might have eternal life" (John 3:16). It was necessary for Jesus to become "the Lamb of God who takes away the sin of the world" (John 1:29). This is what makes the sacrifice of Jesus essential. It is essential in that it is the only means that God has established for our salvation. If we could have saved ourselves through our own efforts and good works, then Jesus would not have had to die the sacrificial death on the Cross. St. Paul explained it this way: "I do not nullify the grace of God; for if justification comes through the law, then Christ died for nothing" (Galatians 2:21). St. Paul adds: "For by grace you have been saved through faith, and this is not from you; it is the gift of God; it is not from works, so no one may boast" (Ephesians 2:8, 9).

Let's meditate:

1. If there had been another way of saving humanity apart from the painful death of Jesus, do you believe that God would have used it?

2. If we could have saved ourselves with our own works, would the death of Jesus have been necessary?

3. What then should be our response to God's gift of the sacrifice of Jesus on the Cross?

4. Should we try to find our own way to salvation or should we accept the sacrifice Jesus offered on our behalf?

Jesus Submitted to God's Will

"Father, if you are willing, take this cup away from me; still, not my will but yours be done" (v. 42).

Throughout his ministry Jesus taught that he came to do the will of the Father. He explained:

"My food is to do the will of the one who sent me and to finish his work" John 4:34). "I cannot do anything of my own. I judge as I hear, and my judgment is just, because I do not seek my own will but the will of the one who sent me" (John 5:30). "Everything that the Father gives me will come to me, and I will not reject anyone who comes to me" (John 6:37).

Jesus practiced what he preached. He had taught his disciples to pray "Your kingdom come, your will be done on earth as it is in heaven" (Matthew 6:10). As the hour of his crucifixion drew near, everything within his human nature sought to avoid the cruelest form of torture designed by the people of that era. His human instinct of self-preservation told him that he should use everything within his power to escape that torturous ordeal. In the final analysis, however, Jesus submitted his will to the will of his heavenly Father. Accepting the will of God led Jesus to the Cross and dying on the Cross resulted in the salvation of humanity.

Let's Meditate:

1. What is our attitude toward Jesus' decision to do the will of the Father?

2. Are we willing to follow the example of Jesus and pray to God: "Not my will but yours be done?

3. What areas of our lives have we not submitted to the will of God?

Jesus Trusted God Completely

> "Father, if you are willing, take this cup away from me; still not my will but yours be done" (v. 42).

It is truly inspiring and reassuring to see that even while Jesus was facing the most crucial experience of his earthly existence, he never wavered for a moment in terms of his relationship to his heavenly Father. The use of the word "Father" (Abba in Aramaic) conveys a total and complete confidence in God. "Even in this terrible hour, when God was making this terrible demand, God was *Father*."[2] Jesus trusted his heavenly Father in every experience of life. Even in the moments when he did not fully understand everything, he trusted his heavenly Father implicitly and never ceased to call him "Father." The sacrifice of Jesus on the Cross, motivated by God's love, resulted in the greatest blessing that we as human beings can ever receive.

Let's Meditate:

1. Do we trust God in every situation in life?

2. When we face the greatest trials and sorrows, can we still call him "Father?"

3. Do we have the assurance that our heavenly Father is always with us no matter what happens in life?

Bible Memory Verse:

"Father, if you are willing, take this cup away from me; still, not my will but yours be done" (Luke 22:42).

Prayer:

"Our Father who art in heaven, hollowed be Thy name. Thy kingdom come, Thy will be done on earth as it is in heaven." I thank you God, from the bottom of my heart, for the privilege I have of calling you "Father."

End Notes

[1] William Barclay, *The Gospel of Mark*, (Philadelphia: The Westminster Press, 1956), 361.

[2] Ibid., 362.

ɪ

Scourging of Jesus at the Pillar
(Matthew 27:11-26)

Jesus endured both spiritual suffering as well as physical suffering prior to and during his death on the cross. The heart of Jesus had undoubtedly been broken by several events that took place before his crucifixion. First, there was the betrayal of Judas. When Judas approached him, Jesus said to him: "Judas, are you betraying the Son of Man with a kiss?" (Luke 22:48) Second, there was the abandonment by his disciples. "Then all the disciples left him and fled" (Matthew 26:56). Third, there was Peter's denial. Earlier Peter had said: "Even though I should have to die with you, I will not deny you" (Matthew 26:35). Later that same evening, however, Peter said before a crowd of bystanders: "I do not know the man" (Matthew 26:74). There was yet another heart breaking event that brought sorrow to his heart, his rejection by Pilate and by the multitude.

The Rejection of Jesus

Rejection by Pilate

As Governor, Pilate had the opportunity to put his trust in Jesus as his Savior and to prevent the execution of Jesus on the Cross.

Pilate's Curiosity

Jesus was arraigned before the procurator, who questioned him: "Are you the king of the Jews?" (Matthew 27:11).

At first it appears as though Pilate is sincerely trying to learn more about Jesus. His question: "Are you the king of the Jews?" implies that Pilate had some notions about the Messianic expectations of the Jewish people. Pilate may have been genuinely interested in finding out if Jesus was the Messiah. While others are mocking, Pilate shows Jesus some respect by talking with him privately and giving him an opportunity to speak for himself. There was undoubtedly something about the demeanor of Jesus that signaled to Pilate that Jesus was different from any other person he had met. Pilate said to him:

"Do you not hear how many things they are testifying against you? (v.13). "But he did not answer him one word, so that the governor was greatly amazed" (v. 14).

Pilate's Caution

In addition to the inner feeling that Jesus was different from all others, Pilate got a word of caution from his wife concerning Jesus. Through dreams it had been revealed to her that Jesus was a "holy man."

"While he was still seated on the bench, his wife sent him a message, 'Have nothing to do with that righteous man. I suffered much in a dream today because of him'" (Matthew 27:19). Pilate's wife did not fully understand the implications of this dream. She did, however, know enough to warn her husband that Jesus was not being treated appropriately.

Pilate's Conclusion

Pilate listened to all of the accusation brought to him by the religious authorities. He also heard them say that they wanted Jesus to be crucified. All of this, however, did not convince Pilate that Jesus was worthy of death. During the trial of Jesus, Pilate stated three times that Jesus was not guilty. First, he said: "I find this man not guilty" (Luke 23:4). Second, he stated: "You brought this man to me and accused him of inciting the people to revolt. I have conducted my investigation in your presence and have not found this man guilty of the charges you have brought against him, nor did Herod, for he sent him back to us. So there has been no capital crime committed by him. Therefore I shall have him flogged and then release him" (Luke 23:14). It is evident that Pilate was convinced that Jesus had not done anything worthy of being crucified.

Pilate's Compromise

In his effort to try to help Jesus, Pilate sought to find a way to release Jesus without assuming personal responsibility for his decision. "Now on the occasion of a festival the prosecutor was accustomed to release a prisoner, whom the crowd would designate. They had at that time a notorious prisoner named Barabbas. Since they were already assembled, Pilate said to them, 'Which one do you want me to release to you, Barabbas, or Jesus called Messiah?'"(v.17). Pilate was wishing that somehow the multitude would choose Jesus (v. 20). This would give him an opportunity to release Jesus, without having to take a stand personally for Jesus. When this did not work, "he took water and washed his hands in the sight of the crowd, saying, 'I am innocent of this man's blood'" (v.24).

Let's meditate:

To what extent does Pilate's attitude toward Jesus resemble ours?

1. Are we merely curious about Jesus?

2. Have we concluded that he is truly the Son of God?

3. Have we compromised our stand toward Jesus because of pressure from those around us?

4. Have we accepted Jesus as our Savior knowing that he died on the cross for us?

Rejection by the Crowd

Like Pilate, the people in the crowd had an opportunity to receive Jesus as their Messiah. At least some of them had seen evidence of the miracles Jesus had performed. The people in the crowd, however, did not think for themselves and did not make an effort personally to discover who Jesus was. They allowed themselves to be influenced by the religious leaders who had already rejected Jesus in their hearts. "The chief priests and the elders persuaded the crowds to ask for Barabbas and but to destroy Jesus "(v. 20). "So when the procurator asked them, 'Which one of the two do you wish me to release to you?' They answered, 'Barabbas!' Pilate said to them, 'Then what shall I to do with Jesus called Messiah?' 'They all said, 'Let him be crucified!'" (vv. 21, 22).

It is very sad to know that, influenced by the religious leaders, the crowd asked for the release of one who had done precisely what they had accused Jesus of doing. Barabbas had been thrown in prison for insurrection (Mark 15:7). In addition to this, Barabbas had committed a murder (Mark 15:7). The crowd chose an insurrectionist and murderer instead of Jesus.

Let's Meditate:

To what extent does the attitude of the crowd toward Jesus resemble ours?

1. Have we allowed others to determine for us who Jesus really is?

2. Have we taken it upon ourselves to study the word of God to know who Jesus is and what his death on the Cross means to us?

3. Do we allow those around us to influence us in the decisions we make about Jesus?

4. Are we ready to recognize that Jesus really is the King of Kings, Lord of Lords and our personal Savior?

Jesus suffered profound spiritual grief brought about by the betrayal of Judas, the abandonment of his disciples, the denial of Peter, the rejection of Pilate, and the rejection of the crowd. In addition to his spiritual suffering, there was immense physical suffering.

Jesus Scourged At the Pillar

In a final effort to release Jesus, Pilate scourged him. His idea was that if he could humiliate Jesus and show the crowd how ridiculous it was to think of Jesus as their king, they would get the point and be satisfied with having Jesus punished (John 19:5). This only angered the crowd even more and they shouted, "Crucify him! Crucify him!"(v.6). While it might appear that scourging Jesus might be only a minor punishment this was not the case at all. Scourging was a severe form of punishment. Barclay explains:

> "The Roman scourge was a terrible thing. The criminal was bent and bound in such a way that his back was exposed. The scourge was a long throng, studded here and there with sharpened pieces of lead and bits of bone. It literally tore a man's back into ribbons. Sometimes it tore a man's eye out. Some men died under it. Some men emerged from the ordeal raving mad. Few retained consciousness under it. It was that that they did to Jesus."[1]

Predicting the severe beating that Jesus was going to suffer on our behalf, Prophet Isaiah had said:

> "But he was pierced by our offenses, crushed for our sins, upon him was the chastisement that makes us whole, by his stripes we were healed" (Isaiah 53: 5).

Let's Meditate:

What does the intense suffering of Jesus, including the scourging he endured, mean to us?

1. Are we grateful to Jesus for the suffering he went through on our behalf?

2. Are we convinced that because of his suffering Jesus is able to understand us when we suffer?

3. Do we feel confident praying directly to him?

Bible Memory Verse:

"Then what shall I do with Jesus called Messiah?" (Matthew 27:22).

Prayer:

Dear Jesus, I could never repay you for the intense suffering you experienced when you were scourged and when you were rejected. I invite you into my heart and my life. Thank you for hearing my prayer, Amen.

End Notes

[1]   William Barclay, *The Gospel of Mark,* (Philadelphia: Westminster Press, 1956), 337.

CROWNING JESUS WITH THORNS
(Matthew 27:28-29)

The suffering of Jesus continued after Pilate, the governor of Rome, had him scourged and turned over to the soldiers. The Governor's soldiers, hardened by the numerous times in which they had dealt with criminals and insurrectionists decided to humiliate Jesus in every way possible.

"Then the soldiers of the governor took Jesus inside the praetorium and gathered the whole cohort around him. They stripped off his clothes and threw a scarlet military cloak about him. Weaving a crown out of thorns, they placed it on his head, and a reed in his right hand. And kneeling before him, they mocked him, saying 'Hail, King of the Jews!' They spat upon him and took the reed and kept striking him on the head." (Vv.27-30).

The soldiers took Jesus to their barracks and called the rest of their detachment (anywhere from 600 to 1,000 men) to entertain themselves by making a sham king out of Jesus. Everything they did had the symbolism of royalty attached to it, but the way in which they did it was clearly to make fun of Jesus and to debase him. Their orders from Pilate were to let the people know just what kind of a king Jesus was.

The Humiliated King

The Stripping of His Clothes

Taking away a person's clothing stripped him of personal dignity. Jewish people who suffered in concentration camps during World War II later testified that taking away their clothing struck a blow at the very essence of their identity and dignity. For some, it amounted to the very loss of their humanity. If that was true of ordinary persons, it must have been infinitely more humiliating to Jesus who was innocent in every respect and dedicated to imparting dignity and self-worth to every person he met. The soldiers, however, sought to degrade Jesus to the lowest level of decency before executing him.

CHAPTER 13

The Scarlet Cloak

Scarlet was perhaps the closest they could get to purple, the color appropriate for royalty. An old worn out scarlet cloak which probably belonged to one of the soldiers, was thrown around Jesus' shoulders to continue the game of pretending that this battered and despised person was a king. A king, after all, should be dressed in a royal purple mantel. One cannot help but imagine how gruesome this cloak looked as it absorbed the blood that was coming out of Jesus' wounded back. The cloak added to the disgrace and provided the opportunity for the soldiers and those around them to mock Jesus and laugh to their heart's content.

The Crown of Thorns

Every king should have a crown. Why not make one for Jesus if one was not available? The crown itself added fodder for ridicule and mockery. It was not a crown of gold or silver. It was not even a garland or laurel wreath such as the ones that were used to honor the victors in the various sports of that day. Instead it was a crown of thorns very likely improvised from a thorny bush that grew in the courtyard. The crown itself wounded the head of Jesus, inflicted pain, and caused the blood to flow. This disfigured the contused face of Jesus. "He did not appear in the artistic elegance of so many of our great painters but in stark hideousness of brutal reality."[1] What could be more ridiculous than a king with a crown of thorns and a face covered with blood?

The Reed on His Hand

The soldiers placed "a reed in his right hand…" (v. 29)

Every king was supposed to have a scepter. It was a symbol of the king's authority. It was used when the king gave orders. The soldiers, therefore, found a reed somewhere and thrust it into Jesus' right hand. The obvious purpose of this was to make fun of Jesus' authority. How much authority did this king have? When would he give the orders for his legions to come to his rescue? The reed conveyed in a ridiculous and cruel way what these soldiers thought of this king's authority.

The reed was used to inflict additional physical pain. "Afterward they took hold of the reed and kept striking him on the head" (v. 30). Already the thorns on the crown that Jesus wore had made deep gashes into his head and forehead. The blood had continued to cover his contused face. The repeated blows to the head with the reed made the thorns penetrate deeper and the blood flow more profusely.

The Mock Adoration

> "And kneeling before him, they mocked him, saying,
> 'Hail, King of the Jews!'" (v. 29)

"The cutting sarcasm of this adoration was intended to humiliate the soul of Jesus as much as possible."[2] The word "hail" (*kairein* in Greek) was used to salute kings in a respectful and admiring manner. Here it is used in a derisive and humiliating way. People generally dropped to their knees as royal subjects to honor their kings. They also bowed in an attitude of submission to present their requests to their king. In this case, however, they salute and bow not to honor their king but to demonstrate that this condemned Galilean is nothing but a diluted imposter who is about to get his just deserts. Their scorn for Jesus was such that "they spat upon him" (v. 30).

Jesus suffered indescribable physical and spiritual anguish even before he was nailed to the Cross. Some have said that we ought not to dwell too much on the suffering of Jesus. As we study the Bible, however, we cannot possibly have too vivid a picture of the suffering that Jesus experienced on our behalf.

Let's Meditate:

1. Let us think of the fact that Jesus was stripped of his clothing and of his dignity.

2. Let us think of the scarlet cloak that was placed on him and how it was stained with the blood that was pouring out because of the scourging.

3. Let us think of the crown of thorns that was forced on his head and the gashes it made as it penetrated his skin.

4. Let us think of the reed that was placed on his right hand and of the way they mocked him when they called him "King."

5. Let us think of the mock adoration when they bowed down before him and pretending that he was their king.

6. What is our attitude toward Jesus knowing that he suffered all of these afflictions and indignities on our behalf because of his profound love for us?

The Exalted King

When we read of all the physical suffering and humiliation that Jesus went through, we cannot help but thank him from the bottom of our hearts for loving us so much. We cannot even imagine the indescribable suffering that Jesus experienced on our behalf. As we study the Bible about the humiliation of Jesus, however, we must not stop there. The Angel asked the women that were at the grave where Jesus was buried: "Why do you seek the living one among the dead? He is not here, but he has been raised" (Luke 24:5). St. Peter gave a similar message to the crowd that gathered at Pentecost: "Therefore let the whole house of Israel know for certain that God has made him both Lord and Messiah, this Jesus whom you crucified" (Acts 2:36). As believers in Jesus Christ, we have a dual task. On the one hand, we need to do everything we can to have the clearest understanding of and deepest appreciation for the suffering that Jesus experienced when he was crucified. On the other hand, we need to rejoice over the fact that God exalted Jesus and he is now the Exalted King. We need to continue to study what the Bible says about the exaltation of Jesus.

The Bible says:

Have among yourselves the same attitude that is also yours in Christ Jesus, Who though he was in the form of God, did not regard equality with God something to be grasped.

Rather, he emptied himself taking the form of a slave, coming in human likeness; and found human in appearance,

He humbled himself, becoming obedient to death, even death on a cross.

Because of this, God greatly exalted him and bestowed on him the name that is above every name,

That at the name of Jesus every knee should bend, of those in heaven and on earth and under the earth, and every tongue confess that JESUS CHRIST IS LORD, to the glory of God the Father!" (Philippians 2:5-11)

In this and other passages the Bible presents the exalted Christ in a way that is a direct contrast to the humiliated Christ. When he first came to earth, because of his love for us, Jesus "humbled himself obediently accepting even death on a cross." This explains why Jesus allowed himself to be tortured and humiliated at the hands of his captors. Due to the obedience of Jesus, "God greatly exalted him and bestowed on him the name that is above every other name." The exalted Jesus Christ, therefore, is the exact opposite of the humiliated Jesus. The Bible presents the exalted Christ as:

Clothed in Dazzling Clothes

"While he was praying, his face changed in appearance and his clothes became dazzlingly white" (Luke 9:29).

Dressed in a Royal Cloak

"A name was written on the part of the cloak that covered his thigh: King of kings and Lord of Lords" (Revelations 19:16).

Wearing a Gold Crown

"Then as I looked and there was a white cloud, and sitting on the cloud one who looked like a son of man, with a gold crown on his head and a sharp sickle in his hand" (Revelations 14:14).

Holding an Iron Rod

"Then I saw the heavens were opened, and there was a white horse; its rider was called 'Faithful and True.' "He judges and wages war in righteousness... Out of his mouth came a sharp sword to strike the nations. He will rule them with an iron rod, and he himself will tread out in the wine press the wine of the fury and wrath of God the Almighty" (Revelations 19:11, 15,16).

Receiving Genuine Adoration

"I looked again and heard the voices of many angels who surrounded the throne and the living creatures and the elders. They were countless in number, and they cried out in a loud voice: Worthy is the Lamb that was slain to receive power and riches, wisdom and strength, honor and glory and blessing!" (Revelations 5:11, 12)

Let's Meditate:

1. The soldiers inflicted all of these indignities because they were ignorant and did not know who Jesus really was. Through the Bible, today we know who Jesus is. What is our attitude toward him?

2. Jesus loved us so much that he endured torture and humiliation for us. What is our relationship with him?

3. Jesus has been exalted by God. Do we worship him only as the Christ on the Cross or do we also worship him as the Exalted King?

4. Those who knowingly and willfully reject him will receive God's judgment. Instead of a fragile reed Jesus has an iron rod in his hand.

5. The time will come when everyone is going to have to recognize the Lordship of Jesus. Have we received him as our Savior and Lord?

Bible Memory Verse:

"That at the name of Jesus every knee should bend, of those in heaven, and on earth and under the earth, and every tongue confess that JESUS CHRIST IS LORD, to the glory of the Father!" (Philippians 2:10-11)

Prayer:

Dear Jesus, Thank you for suffering such torments and indignities for me. Even though others made fun of you, I accept you as my Lord and King.

End Notes

[1] RCH Lenski, *The Interpretation of St. Matthew's Gospel*, (Minneapolis: Augsburg Publishing House, 1943) 1102.

[2] Ibid.

Carrying the Cross to Calvary
(John 19:17-19)

The suffering of Jesus continued as he made his way to his crucifixion. He had suffered agony at the Garden of Gethsemane as he prayed to the Father and submitted to his will. He had spent all night being interrogated by the Sanhedrin, the supreme court of the Jews. Their goal was to formulate charges against Jesus. Pilate, the Roman governor, then questioned Jesus extensively. From there he was sent to Herod who wanted Jesus to entertain him and those around him by performing a miracle. When Jesus refused, he was then returned to Pilate who was trying to find a way to release him without accepting personal responsibility for his actions. The roar of the crowd, "Crucify him, Crucify him!" convinced Pilate that Jesus needed to be punished. Pilate then ordered the scourging, which reduced Jesus' back to ribbons of wounded bleeding flesh. The soldiers added insult to injury when they put a crown of thorns on his head, a reed on his hand, and an old military cloak on his shoulders to mock the Galilean King. Beating him on the head with the reed and spitting on him, they sought to humiliate Jesus and to inflict upon him the deepest pain possible.

Jesus Carrying the Cross

As if all the suffering Jesus had endured was not enough, he was forced to carry the cross towards the place where he was to be crucified. St. John explains, "carrying the cross himself he went out to what is called the Place of the Skull, in Hebrew, Golgotha" (John 19:17).

Barclay describes what usually took place on the way to a crucifixion:

> The routine of the crucifixion was always the same. When the case had been heard, and the criminal had been condemned, the judge uttered the fateful sentence: "*Ibis ad crucem*," "You will go to the cross." The verdict was carried out there and then. The criminal was placed in the center of a quaternion, a company of four Roman soldiers. His own cross was placed upon his shoulders. It is to be remembered that the scourging always preceded crucifixion,

and it is to be remembered how terrible scourging was. Often the criminal had to be lashed and goaded along the road, to keep his feet, as he staggered to the place of crucifixion. Before him there walked an officer with a placard on which was written the crime for which he was to die. He was led through as many streets as possible on the way to the place of crucifixion... There was a grim reason that as many as possible should see it, and should realize that crime does not pay, and should take warning from such a fate."[1]

Roman laws required a condemned man to carry his cross to the place of execution and no exception was made in the case of Jesus. Crucifixions usually took place outside the city. Prisoners were led through the most populous streets and were executed near a highway where large numbers of people would gather to watch the spectacle. Some of the people were so cruel and blood thirsty that they sought to humiliate and insult condemned men as they carried their cross. There were others, usually relatives and friends, who walked alongside the condemned person and wept in sorrow. This was the case with regards to Jesus. St. Luke explains: "A great crowd of people followed him, including women who beat their breasts and lamented over him" (23:27).

Much has been written about the form of the cross, which Jesus carried. Some contend that it was only the cross-beam that Jesus carried. That would not lend credence to St. John's statement that Jesus "carried the cross" (19:17). Lenski's explanation is more consistent with the biblical account:

> It was neither an X nor a T, but an upright post with a crossbeam a little beneath the top. The two beams were fastened together at the start. All the evidence shows that Jesus was burdened with the entire cross and not merely the upper crosspiece of *patibulum*. Jesus' own act in literally bearing the cross on which he died lends powerful effect to his word about our taking up the cross to bear it after him, (Matthew 10:38; 16:24).[2]

Jesus, the beloved Son of God, carried the cross, the instrument of torture and death on his shoulders as he made his way to the place of execution.

Jesus Unable to Continue Carrying the Cross

"As they led him away, they laid hold of one Simon the Cyrenean who was coming in from the fields" (Luke 23:26).

As we read this description written by St. Luke it is obvious that Jesus was physically unable to carry the cross any further. The beatings he had endured, the loss of blood, the deprivation of food, water, and sleep along with the weight of the cross, had drained every ounce of energy from the body of our blessed Savior. Exhausted, wounded, and burdened he was unable to carry the cross any further. If the regular procedure was followed, the soldiers had repeatedly goaded him with their spears to force him to keep his feet. The time came, however, when it was obvious that there was absolutely no strength left in him and he collapsed to the ground. He, however, was forced to walk in front of Simon on his way to Golgotha.

Let's Meditate:

1. Jesus voluntarily accepted the role of a condemned criminal as he carried the Cross. What is our response to this act of love?

2. Jesus suffered intense pain and humiliation as he made his way to the place where he was crucified. How capable is he to understand us when we go through difficult times in our lives?

3. Jesus used every ounce of his energy as he carried the Cross. How much of our time and energy are we willing to use in order to serve him?

Simon Was Conscripted to Carry the Cross

"They put the cross on Simon's shoulder for him to carry along behind Jesus" (Luke 23:26).

Simon must have been a complete stranger who was returning from "the fields" and was caught in the middle of a crucifixion procession. Roman soldiers had the power to conscript people for the tasks that they wanted done. For Simon, this must have been an extreme annoyance and indignity. He must have hated the Roman soldiers and this criminal whose cross he was being forced to carry. If he was a resident in Jerusalem he may have been going home from work. Very likely he had family and friends waiting for him, but he was forced to join the procession. This would cause a long, unexpected delay on his plans. If he was in Jerusalem for the Passover, he may have come in from Cyrene, Africa at great expense to him. He may have looked forward to fulfilling his life-long ambition of eating the Passover in Jerusalem. Suddenly, however, there was that dreaded tap on the shoulder and the irrevocable order to carry the cross. Aside from this, to touch the cross, the instrument of death, must have been very revolting to Simon, especially since it was Passover time. This would make him ceremonially unclean. Forced to join the condemned man in his journey, Simon also becomes the laughing stock as if he himself were a criminal. Simeon while he was walking behind Jesus carrying his cross made himself look as if he were on the way to his own execution.

What, at first, appeared to be a curse for Simon later became a blessing for him. Simon's initial intention may have been to fling the cross down on the ground and depart as quickly as possible from the scene of the crucifixion. It may be, however, that something happened to Simon as he carried the cross of Jesus. He may have observed that this condemned man was different from all others. He did not curse and complain. Instead he suffered in silence and dignity. Simon also saw the love in the women who were weeping as they accompanied Jesus in the procession. It may also be that Simon lingered at the crucifixion and saw the sacrificial manner in which Jesus died and heard the words of forgiveness that he spoke from the cross. He may have concluded with the Centurion: "Truly, this was the Son of God."

We are not told in a direct manner that Simon became a follower of Jesus Christ. In St. Mark's reference to him, there is a strong implication that Simon did become a disciple of Jesus: "And they impressed into service a man called Simon of Cyrene, who was passing by, on his way from the country, the father of Alexander and Rufus, and they made him carry His cross" (Mark 15:21-28). Describing Simon as "the father of Alexander and Rufus," implies that the readers of Mark's Gospel knew who Alexander and Rufus were. Barclay explains:

> Now such a description must have been meant to identify him. The people for whom the Gospel was written must have been meant to recognize him by description. It is most likely that Mark's gospel was first written for the Church in Rome. Now, let's turn to Paul's letter to Rome and read 16:13. "Salute Rufus, chosen in the Lord, and his mother and mine." Rufus was so choice a Christian that he was *chosen in the Lord*. The mother of Rufus was so dear

126

to Paul that he could call her his own mother, Things must have happened to Simon on Golgotha. Now turn to Acts 13:1. There is a list of the men in Antioch who sent Paul and Barnabas on that epoch-making first mission to the Gentiles. The name of one is Simeon that was called Niger. Simeon is another form of Simon. Niger was the regular name for a man of swarthy skin who came from Africa, and Cyrene is in Africa. Here it may well be that we are meeting Simon again. Maybe it is true that Simon's experience on the way to Golgotha, bound his heart forever and forever to Jesus.[3]

It is very likely that Simon, the stranger from Cyrene, who resented being forced to carry the cross of a condemned Galilean, became a believer in Jesus Christ. He did not just follow him physically as he carried Christ's cross; he followed him spiritually as he carried the cross of discipleship the rest of his life.

We are Invited to Carry Christ's Cross

Jesus said: "If anyone would be my disciple, let him deny himself, take up his cross and follow me" (Matthew 16:24)

What does carrying the cross of Christ mean? Some people find a great source of comfort carrying a beautiful crucifix around their neck. As meaningful and inspiring as this might be, this is not what Jesus meant by carrying his cross. Others feel that any sorrow or burden that they bear is a cross. While it is true that Jesus is concerned about our trials and tribulations, this is not what he meant by carrying his cross. *The cross of Christ is what is borne in the act of confessing him.* When we invite Jesus into our lives as our Lord and Savior we are carrying the cross of Christ. This means that we are committing to become life-long followers of Jesus Christ. This is taking on the cross of discipleship.

Making this decision will bring opposition and criticism from others. When people criticize us or persecute us for our loyalty to Christ, then we are carrying his cross. When we sacrifice and work for Christ and his kingdom, we are carrying his cross. When we take a stand for principle and take the consequences of loss or scorn, because we are followers of Christ, we are carrying his cross. The pain we may feel in speaking to another in Christ's name, the sacrifice of comfort or time we take in engaging in Christian work, the self-denial we exercise in giving of our resources that the Kingdom of Christ may spread at home and abroad, the reproach we may bear in identifying ourselves with Christ or in assisting despised persons because they are on Christ's side, as we do these things we are bearing his cross.

Let's Meditate:

1. *The cross of Christ is what is borne in the act of confessing him.* Have we made a personal and conscious decision to accept Jesus as our Lord and Savior?

   If not, will we do it now?

2. The cross that Jesus wants us to carry is the cross of discipleship. This means that we are willing to become his life-long learners and followers. Are we willing to study the Bible consistently to learn more about Jesus every day?

3. After we have committed our lives to Jesus, we are at times called upon to carry the cross of suffering brought about by those who are not following Jesus. Are we willing to trust Jesus to give us strength to carry his cross with patience and grace?

Bible Memory Verse:

"Whoever wishes to come after me must deny himself, take up his cross, and follow me" (Matthew 16:24).

Prayer:

Dear Jesus, it breaks my heart to know that you had to carry your cross to Calvary. Thank you for being willing to suffer so much to save me. I accept you as my Lord and Savior. Please help me to carry your cross with gratitude and dedication. Thank you for hearing my prayer, Amen.

End Notes

[1]   William Barclay, *The Gospel of John*, Volume 2, (Philadelphia: Westminster Press, 1958), 293

[2]   RCH Lenski, *The Interpretation of St John's Gospel*, (Minneapolis: Augsburg Publishing House, 1942), 1279.

[3]   William Barclay, *The Gospel of Mark, Philadelphia*: (Westminster Press, 1958), 279-80.

THE CRUCIFIXION OF JESUS
(Luke 23:32-49)

On one occasion a missionary was showing a movie about the crucifixion of Jesus to a tribe that had not heard the Gospel. When the moment came in which they nailed the hands of Jesus on the cross, the chief of the tribe ordered them to stop the movie and cried: "Do not put him on the cross! I deserve to be there!"

William Barclay described the crucifixion in the following manner:

> Klausner, the Jewish writer, writing of crucifixion says, "Crucifixion is the most terrible and cruel death which man has ever devised for taking vengeance on his fellow-men." Cicero called it "the most cruel and horrible torture," Tacitus called it "a torture only for slaves." It originated in Persia; and its origin came from the fact that the earth was considered sacred to Ormuzd the god, and the criminal was lifted up from it that he might not defile the earth, which was god's property. From Persia crucifixion passed to Carthage in North Africa; and it was from Carthage that Rome learned it, although the Romans kept it exclusively for rebels, runaway slaves, and the lowest type of criminal. It was indeed a punishment that was illegal to inflict on a Roman citizen. Klausner goes on to describe crucifixion. The criminal was fastened to his cross, already a bleeding mass from the scourging. There he hung to die of hunger and thirst and exposure, unable to defend himself from the torture of gnats and flies, which settled on his naked body and on his bleeding wounds. It was not a pretty picture – but that is what Jesus Christ suffered – willingly, for us.[1]

In the Sacred Scriptures we find a painful and moving description of the events related to the crucifixion of Jesus. At the same time we find there what the crucifixion means for our lives. Will it be possible by reading the Word of God that we will come to the same conclusion as the chief, that Jesus took our place on the Cross?

The Painful Events of the Crucifixion

The death of our Savior Jesus Christ was not instantaneous, but rather consisted of a series of painful events. In each of these events we see evidence of the profound love of Jesus towards us and of his divine character. Let us ask for the presence of God in our hearts as we study these painful events.

Let us pray: "Our Father who art in the heavens, help us to understand the significance of the death of your Son Jesus on the cross. Help us to be attentive to your voice as we study your Holy Word. Amen."

The Suffering of Jesus

Luke explains, "When they came to the place called the Skull, they crucified him" (Luke 23:33). The crucifixion was the cruelest method of torture that the Romans could have designed. First they nailed the hands and the feet of the prisoner. Next they raised the cross, shifting the weight of the body and causing deep pain. Upon losing blood and feeling the burning rays of the sun, the prisoners experienced a great thirst. When the legs lost all strength, the weight of the body fell on the arms, at which time breathing became a struggle. In order to be able to breathe, they made an effort to support their weight with their legs. This agony continued until the person lost all energy and gradually was asphyxiated.

The suffering of Jesus was even deeper than this. He also suffered because the people and the soldiers continued mocking him, (Luke 23:35-37) and because the soldiers cast lots to see to whom his clothes would be left (John 19:23-24). But more than anything, Jesus suffered because he had to carry the sin of all humanity in his body to death on the cross. Because of our sin He felt the separation from God, his Father.

The Words of Jesus from the Cross

On many occasions the words that people say at death reveal their character. This was certainly true in the case of Jesus.

1. The forgiving character of Jesus was revealed when he cried out, "Father, forgive them, they know not what they do" (Luke 23:34). If Jesus forgave those that crucified him, can he forgive me?

2. His compassion was revealed when he said to the repentant prisoner, "Amen, I say to you, today you will be with me in Paradise" (Luke 23:43). Does Jesus have compassion towards me today?

3. The concern of Jesus for the well being of his mother was shown when he said, "Woman, behold, your son' then he said to the disciple, 'Behold, your mother'" (John 19:26). Is Jesus concerned today for our well being?

4. The suffering of Jesus from the interruption of his perfect communion with the Father was seen when he cried out, "My God, my God, why have you forsaken me?" (Matthew 27:46). Does Jesus understand us when we feel abandoned?

5. The suffering of Jesus as a human being was revealed when he moaned, "I thirst" (John 19:28). Does Jesus understand us when we physically suffer?

6. The satisfaction of Jesus having completed his mission was shown when he exclaimed, "It is finished" (John 19:30). Are we convinced that upon completing his mission Jesus did all that was necessary for our salvation?

7. Jesus' complete confidence in God was shown when he prayed, "Father into your hands I commend my spirit" (Luke 23:46). Do we have the same confidence that when our lives end here that we are going to entrust ourselves to God?

The Meaning of the Crucifixion

Without doubt our hearts have been broken studying the painful events of the crucifixion. We cannot contemplate Christ on the cross without asking the question, why did the beloved Son of God have to die? The Word of God answers this question.

CHAPTER 15

The Crucifixion was a Sacrifice

The Word of God says:

> "Yet it was our infirmities that he bore, our sufferings that he endured, while we thought of him as stricken, as one smitten by God and afflicted. But he was pierced for our offenses, crushed for our sins, upon him was the chastisement that makes us whole; by his stripes we were healed. We had all gone astray like sheep, each following his own way; but the Lord laid upon him the guilt of us all." (Isaiah 53:4-6).

The only explanation for the death of Jesus is that on the cross He paid for our sins - yours and mine.

Let us meditate. This portion of the Bible says that Jesus:

1. Bore our _____.

2. Endured our _____.

3. Was pierced for our _____

4. The punishment of our _____fell on him.

5. By his strifes we were _____.

6. The Lord laid on him the _____of all of us.

The Crucifixion was a Complete Sacrifice

When the Lord Jesus was on the cross, he exclaimed, "It is complete." This means that He completed his mission of doing all that was necessary for our salvation. Peter explains, "for Christ also suffered for sins once, the righteous for the sake of the unrighteous, that he might lead you to God. Put to death in the flesh, he was brought to life in the spirit" (I Peter 3:18). "Suffered for sins once," means that:

1. The sacrifice of Jesus was unique. That which Christ did on the cross cannot be repeated or improved.

2. The sacrifice of Jesus was complete. There is nothing that we can add to the sacrifice of Christ in order to receive our salvation.

3. The sacrifice of Jesus was undeserved. Paul clarified this to the believers, who thought that by obeying religious laws they could obtain the justification of God. He told them, "I do not nullify the grace of God; for if justification comes through the law, then Christ died for nothing" (Galatians 2:21). If we could save ourselves by our own efforts or our religious acts, then Christ would not have had to die.

Because the sacrifice of Christ on the cross was complete, what must we do to receive salvation? The answer to this question can be found in that which the criminal on the cross did. Although one criminal and the soldiers were mocking Jesus, the other criminal believed in Jesus and asked of him, "Jesus remember me when you come into your kingdom" (Luke 23:42). Jesus answered him, "Amen, I say to you, today you will be with me today in Paradise" (v.43).

Let's Meditate:

1. What was it that saved the prisoner?

2. Could he do acts of charity?

3. Could he participate in the activities of the church?

4. Did he have to ask others aside from Jesus, to intercede to God on his behalf?

The prisoner could not do religious acts or acts of charity to earn his salvation; he only believed in Christ. Jesus talked of this simple and personal faith when he told Nicodemus, "For God so loved the world that he gave his only Son, so that everyone who believes in him might not perish but might have eternal life" (John 3:16).

Let' Meditate:

1. Do I have that simple faith of the prisoner?

2. Have I recognized that Jesus truly is the Son of God?

3. Have I put all my faith in Him as my Savior?

It is inspiring to meditate on the painful events of the death of Jesus. But this is not enough. In order to apply the significance of the sacrifice of Jesus to our life we need to believe in Him as our Savior. Let us remember, by his pain we receive our healing; by his suffering, our forgiveness; and by his sacrifice, our salvation.

Bible Memory Verse:

"For God so loved the world, that he gave his only Son, so that everyone who believes in him might not perish but might have eternal life" (John 3:16).

Prayer:

Most gracious heavenly Father, thank you for loving me so much that you sent your Son to die on the Cross for my sins. Knowing that I cannot save myself, I put my complete trust in Jesus Christ as my only Savior. Thank you for hearing my prayer, Amen.

End Notes

[1]   William Barclay, *The Gospel of Matthew,* Volume 2, (Philadelphia: Westminster Press, 1958), 401, 02.

PART FOUR:

THE GLORIOUS MYSTERIES

The Rosary does not end with the *Sorrowful Mysteries*. It moves on from the sorrow or the Crucifixion to the joy of the Resurrection. The *Glorious Mysteries* are based on the glorious fact the Jesus did not remain in the tomb but arose from the dead. The women at the tomb heard the message of the angels: "Why do you seek for the living one among the dead? He is not here, but he has been raised" (Luke 24:5-7). After his resurrection, Jesus appeared to his disciples "during forty days and speaking about the kingdom of God" (Acts 1:3).

Having completed his ministry on earth, Jesus ascended into heaven. "As they were looking on, he was lifted up, and a cloud took him from their sight" (Acts 1:9). The ascended Jesus, however, did not leave his disciples comfortless. He sent his Holy Spirit to be with them (John 14:18,25,26). Jesus promised his disciples that they would have an advocate who would comfort and guide them. The descent of the Holy Spirit, therefore, was the fulfillment of that promise. At his ascension, Jesus made yet another promise "I will come back to you" (John 14:3,28). Based on this promise, the *Mystery of Christ's Return* has been included among the *Glorious Mysteries* that are clearly and emphatically taught in the Bible. The *Glorious Mysteries*, therefore, focus not only on the glorious events connected with the Resurrection of Jesus', the Ascension of Jesus, and the Descent of the Holy Spirit, but on the fulfillment of Jesus promise that he would return to take true believers to be with him (John 14:1-4).

During his earthly ministry Jesus made it very clear that only those who receive him as Lord and Savior will go to be in heaven with him. He told Nicodemus: "I say to you, no one can see the kingdom of God without being

137

born from above"(John 3:3). He told the Samaritan woman: "God is Spirit, and those who worship him must worship in Spirit and truth" (John 4:24). In order to assure us that if we repent we can count on God to forgive and restore us, he told the parable of the Prodigal Son (Luke 15:11-24). Through the parable of the Rich Man and Lazarus, Jesus taught that while we are still alive we decide our eternal destiny (Luke 16:19-31). These teachings have been included to help us to be ready to meet God when he calls us. As we reflect on the Glorious Mysteries found in the Bible, let us have confidence that our Advocate, the Holy Spirit, is with each repentant individual and anticipate that at the appointed time, Jesus is coming back to take us with him.

THE RESURRECTION OF CHRIST
(Luke 23-24)

Upon meditating on the painful events related to the death of Jesus, our hearts are filled with sorrow. The agony in the garden, the flagellation, the coronation of thorns, the cross on his back, and the crucifixion help us to understand how much our Lord Jesus Christ suffered in order to make our salvation possible. It is very important, nevertheless, that our understanding of Jesus does not end with his death on the cross. The truth is that God raised him, and this has great significance for our lives.

The resurrection of Jesus is the most glorious event of Christianity. In the Sacred Scriptures we find equally as much clear and convincing evidence of the resurrection as we find evidence of the significance of this glorious event for our lives.

The Evidence of the Resurrection

In the Bible there is abundant evidence that Christ did not stay dead in the tomb, but rather that he was raised. Let us ask God to illumine our mind upon examining this evidence.

The Evidence of the Empty Tomb

In the gospel according to Luke we read of the ladies that had followed him from Galilee (Mary Magdalene, Joanna, Mary the mother of Jacob and others). "On the first day of the week, they took the spices they had prepared and went to the tomb" (Luke 24:1). On arriving there, they found two surprises. First, "they found the stone rolled away from the tomb" (v.2). Second, "when they entered, they did not find the body of the Lord Jesus" (v.3). Being worried, thinking about what had happened with the body of Jesus, they saw two angels who said to them, "Why do you seek the living one among the dead? He is not here, but he has been raised" (v. Vv.5-6). Not only did the women find the tomb empty, Peter also "ran to the tomb, bent down, and saw the burial cloths alone; then he went home amazed at what had happened" (v.12). If the Jewish leaders could have found the body of Jesus, they would have put it in a public place to prove to the people that the disciple's message, that Jesus had been raised, was a lie. But they never could find the body because indeed Jesus arose from the tomb.

Let us meditate:

1. We are accustomed to seeing the crucifixes (with Jesus on the cross), but are we aware that Christ did not remain on the cross?

2. What does the fact that the tomb was empty mean for us?

3. Intellectually we recognize that Christ rose, but emotionally, do we feel his presence in our life each day?

The Evidence of the Appearances of Christ

In the Sacred Scripture we find clear and convincing evidence that the tomb was empty. This in itself does not mean that Christ rose. But we have more evidence of the different occasions on which Christ presented himself before his followers, talked with them, permitted them to touch him, and brought them together to see him go up to heaven. Let us review briefly these occasions:

1. Christ presented himself to Mary Magdalene (Mark 16:9-11; John 20:11-18);

2. He presented himself to the ladies that were returning from the grave (Matthew 28:5-10);

3. He presented himself to Peter (Luke 24:34: I Corinthians 15:5);

4. He presented himself to the two disciples that were going on route (the road) to Emmaus (Mark 16:12-13; Luke 24:13-35);

5. He presented himself to ten of the disciples that were together in the high room (upper room) (John 20:19-20);

6. He presented himself to the disciples when Thomas was present (John 20:24-29; Mark 16:14);

7. He presented himself to James (I Corinthians 15:7);

8. He presented himself to the disciples together at the Sea of Galilee (John 21:1-14);

9. He presented himself to the eleven disciples on the Mount of Galilee and gave them the command to preach the gospel to all the world (Matthew 28:16-20)

10. He presented himself to more than 500 at one time (I Corinthians 15:6);

11. He met with his disciples in Bethany and in the sight of all, was carried into heaven (Luke 24:50-53); (Mark 16:19-20); (Acts 1:9-11).

As we can see, the descriptions of the appearances of Jesus were not inventions of someone, instead they were the testimony of people that saw him, touched him and talked with him. They were not only the apostles, but also simple people like Mary Magdalene, who gave the news of the resurrection of Jesus. It would be erroneous to say that the people were imagining that Christ had risen. In the first place, it was not only one or two people that saw him but rather the apostles, other disciples, and on one occasion more than 500 at one time. What is more, they did not see him only for one day, instead he continued to show himself for 40 days. Jesus did not present himself in only one place but instead in many places and in different situations. Mary Magdalene was crying, Thomas was filled with doubts, the disciples who were walking to Emmaus were totally confounded, and the eleven disciples were filled with fear. In each one of these circumstances, they were convinced that the Christ, that had died on the cross and had been buried, now was before them filled with life and with the glory of God. The appearances of Christ in different places, different occasions, to different people for a period of 40 days left his followers completely convinced that he fulfilled his promise of rising on the third day (Luke 9:22; 18:31-34).

Let us meditate:

There is a difference between the appearances of Christ and the apparitions that some say that they have seen. An apparition can be the result of the imagination, while a bodily appearance is physical and real.

Let us review:

The appearances of Christ:

1. Were in different _____.

2. Were to different _____(to more than 500 people).

3. Were throughout 40 days.

4. Were physical - the disciple touched him (see Matthew 28:9 and John 20:27).

5. Were in order to direct attention toward God.

6. Were in agreement with the Word of God.

These appearances were verified and not the product of the imagination nor of the hallucinations of some people. The Christ that died was the same that rose and that presented himself to his followers.

The Evidence of the Changed Lives of the Disciples

One of the most powerful evidences of the resurrection of Jesus is the change that occurred in the lives of the disciples when they saw Christ risen. When Christ died, his disciples felt disillusioned, sad and afraid. The Messiah in whom they had put all their faith had been crucified, and with the death of Jesus all of their hopes had died. But when they saw Christ risen, all this changed. With great joy and enthusiasm they ran to tell the others that Christ had been raised from the dead.

The fact, which convinces us that they were completely sure that they had seen the risen Christ, was that they were willing to die for him after giving this testimony. Peter and John, for example, after having performed a miracle of healing a paralytic, were threatened by the authorities that if they talked about the risen Christ they would be thrown in prison. With great courage they answered the authorities:

> "Then all of you and all the people of Israel, should
> know that it was in the name of Jesus Christ the Nazarean

whom you crucified, whom God raised from the dead; in his name this man stands before you healed. Whether it is right in the sight of God for us to obey you rather than God, you be the judges. It is impossible for us not to speak about what we have seen and heard" (Acts 4:10, 19-20).

If they were not completely convinced that Christ had been risen, do you believe that they would have been willing to give their life for proclaiming the message?

The evidence of the resurrection of Jesus is clear and convincing. The tomb was empty; they could never find the dead body of Jesus. Christ appeared to his followers repeatedly for 40 days. This was not the illusion of one or two people because more than 500 people saw him, talked with him, and listened to his teachings. Added to this, his followers were changed from discouraged disciples to motivated missionaries. They were so convinced that the risen Christ had sent them to preach his message of salvation that many of them gave their lives to fulfill with this command.

Let us meditate:

The changed lives of the followers of Christ were evidence of his resurrection.

1. Have I noticed the change in some people that have invited Christ into their heart?

2. Have I invited Christ to come to my heart and change my life?

3. Is there something in my life that I especially desire for Christ to change?

The Significance of the Resurrection

The descriptions of the resurrection of Jesus (the empty tomb, his appearances and the changed lives) are of great importance because they help us to know that our faith is based on historical events. It was something that truly happened and not something that someone imagined. But so that all of this will not only be a nice story of something that happened in the past, we need to ask ourselves the question, what does the resurrection of Jesus mean to me on this day? In other words, where is Christ risen today?

143

Today Christ is with Those Who Have Lost Hope

In Luke 24:15-24 we find the description of two disciples that were going from Jerusalem to Emmaus. Their hearts were filled with sorrow because Christ, whom they had loved so much, had been executed in the cruelest way that had been invented. Along with Christ's death, their hopes that they had of Him liberating them from the oppression of the Romans, had died (v.21). It was on that sad and solitary path that Christ appeared and reminded them of his promises (v.25-31). Upon giving them the account that the risen Christ had appeared before them, they said, "Were not our hearts burning within us while he spoke to us on the way and opened the scriptures to us?" (v.32). They returned to Jerusalem to tell the news.

When we, due to the circumstances, the disappointments and the sufferings of life, have lost hope, we can rely on the presence of Christ. He says in his Word, "I came so that they might have life, and have it more abundantly" (John 10:10). This life is full of joy and hope because He is with us. With Jesus in our heart we can approach life with confidence. Because of this Paul says, "I have the strength for everything through him who empowers me" (Philippians 4:13).

Let us meditate:

1.   Have I lost hope with respect to some things in my life?

2.   Do I desire to invite Christ so that he will bring hope to my life?

Today Christ is with Those Who Need His Forgiveness

In Matthew 26:69-75 we find the narration of the occasion in which Peter denied that he knew Jesus. The soldiers had arrested Jesus. Peter came close to a courtyard where people were warming themselves next to the fire. When a servant said that Peter was a follower of Jesus, he denied it and even used bad words to prove that he did not know him. At that moment, Jesus went by there and heard Peter's denial. When Peter realized the sin that he had committed, "he began to weep bitterly" (Luke 22:61-62). It is very encouraging to see that when the risen Christ told the women to tell the news of his resurrection, he instructed them specifically that they tell Peter (Mark 16:7). Because Peter repented, Jesus forgave him.

When we have sinned against God, against our loved ones and against ourselves, we need the forgiveness of Jesus. John says that if we confess our sins, "he is faithful and just and will forgive our sins and to cleanse us from every wrongdoing " (I John 1:9).

Let us meditate:

1. Do I need the forgiveness of Christ today?

2. Am I willing for him to come into my life and forgive my sins?

Today Christ is with Those Who Have Doubts

In John 20:24-29 we find the experience of Thomas. He had heard that Jesus had arisen, but he had not seen him. For that reason he refused to believe (v.25). But eight days later, Jesus appeared to Thomas and the others and told them, "Put your finger here and see my hands, and bring your hand and put it into my side, and do not be unbelieving, but believe" (v.27). On seeing the evidence, Thomas exclaimed, "My Lord and my God!"(V.28).

Christ is not impatient when we have sincere doubts. If we truly want to know the truth, he is close to us to guide us by means of his Word. He said, "I am the way and the truth and the life. No one comes to the Father except through me" (John 14:6).

Let us meditate:

1. Do I have some doubts with regards to:

2. The teachings of Christ? _____

3. The salvation that Christ offers? _____

4. The Christian life? _____

5. Going to heaven when I die? _____

6. Am I willing to trust in the risen Christ as my personal Savior?

    _____

145

7. The resurrection is more than a historical event; it is a reality in our lives. Have you permitted the living Christ to come to live in your heart?

Bible Memory Verse:

"Jesus said to him, 'I am the way and the truth and the life. No one comes to the father except through me'" (John 14:6).

Prayer:

Dear Heavenly Father, I thank you from the bottom of my heart for raising Jesus from the dead. Help me to live every day with the assurance that the resurrected Jesus lives within my heart and is able to help me overcome any situation that I might face. In Jesus' name I pray, Amen.

THE ASCENSION OF JESUS
(Luke 24 & Acts 1)

After having been raised, Jesus appeared to his followers throughout 40 days. At the end of his earthly ministry, He did not simply disappear. Instead he met with his disciples and said goodbye to them. He wanted to give them final instructions and to give them the opportunity to see the power of God carrying him to heaven. Luke describes this event in two portions of the Bible, Luke 24:50-53 and Acts 1:6-11. This account was very important because it marked the end of the earthly ministry of Jesus and established his heavenly priesthood.

The Ascension of Jesus

The Preparation for the Ascension

Before going up to heaven, Jesus withdrew his disciples from the city of Jerusalem and took them to the mount in Bethany (Luke 24:50). There is no doubt that he wanted to be alone with them, because it would be the last time that they would see him here on the earth. Aware of the shock that they would receive upon his departure, Jesus lifted his hands and blessed them. We do not know what Jesus said to bless them, but we do know that in his prayer for them (John 17), he asked that God:

1. Would guard them from evil (v. 15) - that he would protect them from the power of the devil. Have we asked God to free us from all evil?

2. Would sanctify them with his word (v. 17) - that the Word of God would help them to dedicate themselves to Him. Have we asked God to help us to receive his Holy Word so that our lives would be dedicated to Him?

3. Would give them a spirit of unity (v. 21) - that they would have a spirit of brotherhood. Have we asked God to give us a spirit of unity with all the people that love Him?

4.   Would prepare a place for them in heaven for those that would receive his Son Jesus Christ in their heart. Do we have assurance that we are going to be with Christ when we die?

As parents give a blessing to their children upon leaving the home, Jesus gave a very special blessing to his disciples.

The Event of the Ascension

Luke explains: "as he blessed them he parted from them and was taken up to heaven" (Luke 24:51). In the book of Acts, Luke adds more detail when he says, "When he said this, as they were looking on, he was lifted up, and a cloud took him from their sight." (Acts 1:9). As we have already said, Christ did not simply disappear without being seen again. He gave to his disciples the privilege of hearing his final words, of receiving his blessing, and of seeing him go up into heaven. Through this miracle of the ascension, his disciples could see the body of Jesus visibly rise higher and higher until the cloud covered him. No other farewell has had the effect of this glorious farewell.

The Significance of the Ascension

Upon reading the description of this event we know what happened - Christ went up into heaven. By examining these and other passages of the Scripture, we are given the account of the significance of the event.

What it Meant for Jesus

For Jesus this event had a significance of the highest importance. His ascension meant the end of his earthly suffering and the beginning of his heavenly coronation. He had completed his mission of:

1.   Being born in this world
2.   Living a holy life
3.   Communicating to people the message of the love of God
4.   Dying on the cross for our sins
5.   Rising on the third day
6.   Returning with honor and glory to the heavenly Father

This is the heart of the gospel. This clearly explains the mission that our beloved Savior Jesus Christ came to complete. If we believe with all our heart and we receive Christ as our Savior, we have complete assurance that we have received the salvation of our soul.

Let us review, then, these eternal truths:

Do I believe that Jesus Christ, the Son of God:

1. Came to take human form and to be born in this world?

2. Lived a holy life without sin?

3. Died on the cross for my sins?

4. Arose on the third day?

5. Returned with honor and glory to the heavenly Father?

On rising, he did that which no other religious leader could do. The resurrection confirmed that all his teachings about the heavenly Father were true. The Son of God came to this world with a mission and, having completed it, he returned to his beloved Father.

The Significance for the Disciples

At first sight it would seem that the ascension of Jesus should have been very sad experience. The disciples knew that it was the last time that they were going to see him here on earth. Luke says, nonetheless, that at a time filled with sadness, they worshipped Jesus (Luke 24:52). Upon seeing the angels and on seeing Jesus lifted up to heaven, they knew that they were in the presence of God. This was not a farewell but rather a coronation. In the same way that subjects kneel and render homage to their king when he is crowned, the disciples bowed their heads and worshipped the King of kings and Lord of lords.

It is important that we recognize that only Christ deserves this worship. None of the apostles, as consecrated as they have been, deserves worship (Acts 10:25-26). Jesus Christ, the Son of God, he who gave his life for us, rose and ascended to heaven, is the only one whom we should worship.

"They did him homage and then returned to Jerusalem with great joy, and they were continually in the temple praising God." (Luke 24:52-53). The visible presence of Jesus was no longer with them, but they knew of his

149

triumph, and for that reason they had so much joy. He left in order to be able to be present in their hearts through the Holy Spirit. Now they had Jesus in heaven to care for them, to guide them and to prepare a place for them. For that reason they were in the temple praising and blessing God (v.53).

Let us meditate:

1. In view of the birth, the life, the death, the resurrection, and the ascension of Jesus, does he deserve our highest worship?

2. After Christ went up to heaven, the disciples knew of his victory in their hearts. Do we have his victory and his presence in our hearts today? _____If not, what do we need to do?_____

The Promise of the Return of Jesus

Another reason why the disciples were not sad was that the angels reminded them of the promise of Jesus to return for them. "Men of Galilee, why are you standing there looking at the sky? This Jesus who has been taken up from you into heaven will return in the same way as you have seen him going into heaven" (Acts 1:11). The promise is that Jesus himself will come for his followers - he will not send a messenger - and that he will come in the same way in which he went up in the clouds, accompanied by angels (see Matthew 25:31). It was this promise that gave great confidence and great joy to the disciples of Jesus. We have the same hope.

Let us meditate:

1. What does it mean that Christ is going to return to take his followers to heaven?

    a. That he himself is going to come? (Acts 1:11)

    b. That he is going to take only those who have accepted him as their Savior? (John 3:16-18)

    c. That he is going to take them to heaven so that they can live with Him? (John 14:3)

2. Am I preparing for the day when Christ returns?

3. What do I need to do to be prepared? (John 3:16)

The Ministry of Jesus in Heaven

Jesus finished his earthly ministry in order to begin his heavenly ministry. What is Jesus doing in heaven?

Jesus is Reigning in Heaven

Peter says the following about the ministry of Jesus in heaven, "who has gone into heaven and is at the right hand of God, with angels, authorities, and powers subject to him" (1 Peter 3:22). The expression "the right hand of God" means the place of honor. Kings always put the most important people of the kingdom to the right of their throne. Jesus occupies the most elevated place in heaven apart from God himself. This is the position of authority, for He has command over all the angels in heaven. Jesus is the King of heaven, clothed with power and majesty.

Let us meditate:

1. In light of this biblical teaching, apart from God himself, who has the supreme authority in heaven and on earth? (Matthew 28:18).

2. Does Christ have authority over evil spirits, magicians and sorcerers? (See also I John 4:4).

3. If I invite Christ into my heart, can He defeat all the evil influences in my life?

4. Since Christ completed his mission, was taken to heaven, and is at the right hand of God, who deserves my supreme worship?

Jesus is Interceding for Us in Heaven

Referring to the ministry of Jesus in heaven, Paul says:

"Who will condemn? It is Christ [Jesus] who died, rather, was raised, who also is at the right hand of God, who indeed intercedes for us." (Romans 8:34).

151

Paul states that nobody can condemn those that have entrusted their life to Christ because He has done all that is necessary for their salvation. He not only died, rose, and was crowned by God, he also intercedes (that is to say, makes requests to the Father) for us. We see in this passage the glorious truth that Christ is at the right hand of the Father pleading for us.

The Word of God teaches that:

1. Christ is the person designated by God to intercede for us. "For there is one God. There is also one mediator between God and the human race, Christ Jesus, himself human, who gave himself as ransom for all" (1 Timothy 2:5). The Bible teaches that the only mediator is _____.

2. Let us ask the questions:

    a. Who died on the cross for our sins?

    b. Who rose on the third day?

    c. Who ascended to heaven and was seated at the right hand of God?

    d. Is there any place in the Bible that teaches that God has designated another person as his mediator?

    e. If Jesus Christ is the only mediator, whom do we need to ask to make requests for us?

The Word of God also teaches how we should draw near to Jesus Christ in order for him to plead on our behalf.

> "Therefore, since we have a great high priest who has passed through the heavens, Jesus, the Son of God, let us hold fast to our confession. For we do not have a high priest who is unable to sympathize with our weaknesses, but one who has similarly been tested in every way, yet without sin. So let us confidently approach the throne of grace to receive mercy and to find grace for timely help" (Hebrews 4:14-16).

The good news that the Word of God gives us is that Jesus is our Mediator, our High Priest, in heaven. He is able to sympathize with us because he lived in this world and encountered the struggles, the problems, and the sufferings of this life. For that reason we can approach Jesus confidently, knowing that He is familiar with our situation. As our High Priest in heaven, he makes requests to God for us and encourages us to follow steadfastly in his way until the day in which we are with Him.

Let us meditate:

What does it mean that we should approach Christ confidently in our prayers?

1. That we should ask him with timidity (fear)?

2. That we do not know if he is listening to us?

3. That we do not know if he understands us?

4. That we do not know if he is able to help us?

Another thing that should give us confidence is the knowledge that the sacrifice of Jesus on the cross was complete in every way. The Word of God says:

> "For Christ did not enter into a sanctuary made by hands, a copy of the true one, but heaven itself, that he might now appear before God on our behalf. Not that he might offer himself repeatedly, as the high priest enters each year into the sanctuary with blood that is not his own; if that were so, he would have had to suffer repeatedly from the foundation of the world. But now once for all he has appeared at the end of the ages to take away sin by his sacrifice. Just as it is appointed that human beings die once, and after this the judgment, so also Christ, offered once to take away the sins of many, will appear a second time, not to take away sin but to bring salvation to those who eagerly await him." (Hebrews 9:24-28).

Let us meditate:

The Bible teaches in this passage that:

1. Christ was offered, how many times?

2. Where did Christ enter in order to present himself to God?

3. For whom did Christ enter heaven?

4. To remove whose sins?

5. In order to save whom?

We see, then, that Jesus Christ, the Son of God, made the perfect sacrifice on the cross, rose and later ascended into heaven in order to be our Perfect Priest. He no longer has to be sacrificed over and over again, but rather being sacrificed only one time, he presented himself before God in order to be our priest.

On thinking about the ascension of Jesus, we no longer feel sad. There is great happiness in our heart.

First, we are happy knowing that Christ is no longer suffering, but instead went up into heaven where he was crowned with honor, power, and glory.

Second, we are happy because we know that since Christ ascended into heaven, He can live in our hearts in a spiritual way.

Third, we are happy because we have complete confidence that He is our Mediator, our High Priest, who sympathizes with us, because he knows our human condition. We do not have to spend time looking for other mediators. Nobody else died for our sins, rose on the third day, ascended into heaven, and sat at the right hand of God in order to intercede for us.

Fourth, we are happy because we have the promise that Christ will return for those that have received him in their heart. As he said to the penitent on the cross, "today you will be with me in Paradise" (Luke 23:43); we are assured by his Word that he longs for the day when we will be with him in glory.

Do you have this hope and this confidence of being with Jesus in heaven? If you do not, you can have it by receiving Jesus as you Savior.

Bible Memory Verse:

"This Jesus who has been taken up from you into heaven will return in the same way as you have seen him going into heaven" (Acts 1:11).

Prayer:

Dear Jesus, my heart is full of joy knowing that you are now in heaven reigning and interceding to the Father on my behalf. Because you are my perfect Mediator and High Priest, I have complete confidence that you fully understand everything I go through and you are able to guide every step I take until I go to heaven with you. Thank you, my precious Savior for what you mean to me, Amen.

THE DESCENT OF THE HOLY SPIRIT
(Acts 2)

One of the reasons why the disciples did not feel sad when Christ went up into heaven was that He promised them that he would not leave them orphans. He told them:

> "And I will ask the Father, and he will give you another Advocate to be with you always, the Spirit of truth, which the world cannot accept, because it neither sees nor knows it. But you know it, because it remains with you, and will be in you." (John 14:16-17).

Jesus considered the presence of the Holy Spirit so important in the lives of his disciples that he commanded them that they not leave Jerusalem until they received him in their heart (Acts 1:4). If Jesus taught that the Holy Spirit was absolutely necessary in the lives of his disciples, it is important for us to study what the Word of God says about the Holy Spirit, the third person of the Holy Trinity. Let us give our attention, then, to the coming of the Holy Spirit and to his ministry in our life.

The Coming of the Holy Spirit

In the book of Acts, Luke explains that the disciples and other followers of Jesus (120 in number) obeyed his command and returned to Jerusalem (Acts 1:12, 15). They "all devoted themselves with one accord to prayer" (1:14) until the day of Pentecost came (2:1). Being together there, praying to God, the Holy Spirit came in a miraculous way.

The Holy Spirit Came From Heaven

The coming of the Holy Spirit was accompanied by a sound "like a strong driving wind" (Acts 2:2). This wind came from heaven and filled the house where they were. In his conversation with Nicodemus, Jesus compared the Holy Spirit with the wind. "The wind blows where it wills, and you can hear the sound it makes, but you do not know where it comes from or where it goes; so it is with everyone who is born of the Spirit" (John 3:8). The fact that we do not see the wind does not mean that it does not exist. Although we do not see it, we can see the result of the wind, and in the same way we can see the change that the Holy Spirit can make in our lives.

Let us meditate:

1. Do we believe in the Holy Trinity - the Father, the Son, and the Holy Spirit? _____

2. If we believe in the Holy Spirit, what place does he occupy in our life? _____

3. Do we understand the role that the Holy Spirit must play daily in our life? _____

The Holy Spirit Filled the Hearts of the Disciples

Not only was the presence of the Holy Spirit felt in the house where they were, but he also became present in the hearts of the disciples. The Word of God says that, "they were all filled with the Holy Spirit" (Acts 2:4). As we already read in John 14:17, Christ told them that the Holy Spirit "remains with you, and will be in you." The Holy Spirit had already been preparing the way for the arrival of Jesus as seen in the annunciation and the birth of Jesus and for the ministry of Jesus as observed in his baptism.

Upon Jesus' going up into heaven, he could no longer be with them in a physical form. They were no longer going to see him, touch him, and hear him. But the miracle was that through the Holy Spirit, now Jesus was going to live in their hearts. In whatever place that they were or in whatever situation, Christ would be with them in a spiritual form through the dwelling of his Spirit in their hearts. This was what gave his disciples valor, comfort, strength, and joy. The marvel of this is that the same can occur in our lives upon receiving Jesus in our heart.

The Holy Spirit Distributed as Tongues of Fire

As surprising, as the sound of the wind, was the miracle of the tongues as of fire that landed on each of them (Act 2:3). In addition to hearing something extraordinary, they saw something extraordinary. Upon the head of each one of them a small flame appeared as a sign. This was the symbol that the Holy Spirit was with them.

But not only was this sign seen, another miracle also occurred. Those who received the Holy Spirit began to preach the Word of God in languages, other tongues that they themselves were not familiar with, but that the strangers that were there from many countries could understand (2:4-12). Upon seeing this miracle, 3000 people repented, received Christ in their heart, were baptized and were added to the group of his followers (2:41).

The coming of the Holy Spirit was a miraculous event. The mighty wind, the tongues of fire, and the ability of sharing the message of God in different languages were a true miracle. The result of all this was that the Holy Spirit came to live in the hearts of the followers of Jesus with the end result being that they did not feel alone, but rather that they had his presence, his comfort, and his direction in their life.

The Ministry of the Holy Spirit in Our Life

The coming of the Holy Spirit was the fulfillment of a promise that Christ made to his disciples, which we find in John 14:15-26 and 16:7-15. These passages explain the ministry of the Holy Spirit in our life.

The Holy Spirit is Our Helper

Jesus said to his disciples, "and I will ask the Father, and he will give you another Advocate to be with you always" (John 14:16). The word that is used for "Advocate" is the word *Paraclete*, which describes one who has been called to be at our side in order to help us. Other words that are used to describe a "Paraclete" are Helper, Defender, Aid, Intercessor or Comforter. The Greeks used the word "Paraclete" to describe a person that was called in order to: (1) testify on behalf of someone in a court; (2) give advice in a difficult situation; (3) help someone that was in danger; (4) encourage persons that felt alone, depressed, and discouraged. The word *Paraclete* describes the ministry of the Holy Spirit in our life. He defends us, counsels us, helps us and encourages us to live the kind of life that Christ wants us to live and to be able to do his holy and divine will.

The Spirit is Our Teacher

Jesus said to his disciples, "The Advocate, the Holy Spirit that the Father will send in my name—he will teach you everything and remind you of all that I told you" (John 14:26). This does not mean that we do not have to go to school to learn reading, mathematics, etc. What it does mean is that the Holy

159

Spirit helps us to understand what Christ taught. We notice that Jesus said that the world does not know the Holy Spirit (John 14:17). The person who does not have the Holy Spirit in his heart cannot understand the teachings of Jesus. Conversely, when the Holy Spirit lives in the heart of a person, He helps him to understand and to obey the beautiful teachings of Jesus.

Christ also said, "When the Advocate comes whom I will send you from the Father, the Spirit of truth that proceeds from the Father, he will testify to me" (John 15:26). When a person listens to the gospel, the good news that Christ died to save us from our sins, arose, ascended into heaven, and is at the right hand of God interceding for us, there is something that says in his or her heart that this is truth, and that he or she should receive Christ. This voice is the voice of the Holy Spirit that testifies about Jesus. He testifies that what the Word of God says about Him is pure truth.

The Holy Spirit is Our Guide

The work of the Holy Spirit is to guide us to God. How can the Holy Spirit do this when there are many people that do not believe that they need Christ in their life? Jesus answers this question when he says, "And when he comes (the Holy Spirit), he will convict the world in regard to sin and righteousness and condemnation" (John 16:8).

The Holy Spirit Guides Us Toward God to Convict Us of Sin

Jesus explains that this guidance is of the Holy Spirit, "sin, because they do not believe in me" (v.9). When the Jews crucified Jesus, they did not believe that they were sinning. But on the day of Pentecost, when they heard the message about the crucifixion, they felt great sadness and remorse (Acts 2.37). As a result of the work of the Holy Spirit, they recognized their sin. The Holy Spirit helps us to recognize that we have sinned against God and he puts in us the desire to repent and be reconciled with God.

The Holy Spirit Guides Us Toward God
to Convict Us of Righteousness (v. 10)

Because God is a holy and just God, he demands that justice be done when a sin has been committed. But the truth is that there is nothing that we can do to deserve the forgiveness of God (Isaiah 64:6); otherwise Christ would not have had to die. The Holy Spirit convinces us that Christ died on the cruel cross for our sins and in this way we are declared righteous before

God. "Therefore, since we have been justified by faith, we have peace with God through our Lord Jesus Christ," (Romans 5:1).

The Holy Spirit Guides Us to Recognize the Justice of God

Throughout his ministry in our life, the Holy Spirit convinces us that the judgement day is coming. There are people who live as if they will never have to give an account for their actions. The Holy Spirit convinces us that one day we are going to be in the presence of the heavenly Judge to give account of all that we have thought, said and done. Hebrew 9:27 says, "Just as it is appointed that human beings die once, and after this the judgment." For those that have not received Jesus Christ as their Savior, this day of Judgement will be a fearsome day. But for the persons that have repented of their sins and have received Christ as their Savior, there will be no fear because He has already declared them righteous before God.

On Judgement Day, the people will not be condemned simply for the sins that they committed, but rather because they refused to receive the sacrifice of Christ on the cross and to believe in Him as their Savior. Jesus said, "And this is the verdict, that the light came into the world, but people preferred darkness to light, because their works were evil" (John 3:19). And later he added, "Whoever believes in the Son has eternal life, but whoever disobeys the Son will not see life, but the wrath of God remains on him" (John 3:36). Paul adds, "Hence, now there is now no condemnation for those who are in Christ Jesus. For the law of the spirit of life in Christ Jesus has freed you from the law of sin and death," (Romans 8:1-2).

The Holy Spirit is the Counselor (Advocate) Paraclete that Christ sent us so that he would come and dwell in our heart. The ministry of the Holy Spirit is to convict us of sin, of righteousness, and of justice. When we obey his voice and we receive Christ in our heart, we have his presence with us in all the circumstances of life and the assurance that we will be with Him when he calls us.

Bible Memory Verse:

"Hence, now there is no condemnation for those who are in Christ Jesus. For the law of the spirit of life in Christ Jesus has freed you from the law of sin and death." (Romans 8:1-2).

161

Prayer:

Dear Jesus, I thank you for making provision for us when you returned to heaven by sending us your Holy Spirit. I thank you that the Holy Spirit is my Advocate, my Counselor, my Intercessor, my Teacher, and my Guide. Help me to know that I am never alone, because your Holy Spirit is always with me. Thank you for the confidence, peace, and joy that this assurance brings to my heart, Amen.

THE RETURN OF JESUS
(Acts 1, Thessalonians 4)

The Bible not only teaches that Jesus died, rose, ascended into heaven and sent the Holy Spirit, but that He will return to this world to take those that have received him as Savior and Lord.[1] Let us remember that when Jesus ascended into heaven, the angels announced, "This Jesus who has been taken up from you into heaven, will return in the same way as you have seen him going into heaven," (Acts 1:11). The apostle Paul also affirms that Christ will return (1 Thessalonians 4:13-17).

What the Return of Christ will be Like

The return of Christ will be personal, unexpected, visible, and accompanied by great symbols of majesty.

The Coming of Christ will be Personal

The passage in 1 Thessalonians 4 says "the Lord himself" (v.16). The message of the angels was, "this Jesus" (Acts 1:11). This affirms what Jesus himself said: "And if I go and prepare a place for you, I will come back again and take you to myself," (John 14:3). Here it is very clear that Christ does not say that he is going to send someone for his chosen ones. He says that He himself is going to prepare the place and that He himself is going to return for his own to take them to where He is. The phrase *I will come* indicates that he that is speaking is he that is going to return. The expressions "I am going to prepare a place for you", and "I will come back again and take you to myself," also indicate that this action will be taken by the one that is speaking; I *am going to prepare a place and I will come back*. Christ will return personally. Nothing apart from his personal return fulfills the promise of Jesus himself and his angels.

Let us meditate:

1. The prophecies given more than 500 years before the first coming of Jesus were fulfilled exactly:

    a. That he was going to be born of a virgin (Isaiah 7:14)

    b. That he was going to be born in Bethlehem (Micah 5:2)

    c. That he was going to die for our sins (Isaiah 53:5)

2. Do we believe that the prophecies about the Second Coming of Christ will also be fulfilled?

3. When Christ promised that he would send the Holy Spirit (the Advocate Counselor), he made it very clear that it would be the Counselor/Advocate and not Christ himself (John 16:7). Do we believe that if Christ promised that He would himself return that he will fulfill his promise?

The Coming of Christ will be Unexpected

Throughout the Bible we find passages that talk about the unexpected way in which Christ will return. He says, "Therefore, stay awake! For you do not know on which day your Lord will come. So too, you also must be prepared, for at an hour you do not expect, the Son of Man will come." (Matthew 24:42,44).

In several passages the expression "like a thief" is used to describe the unexpected way in which Christ will return. Peter says, "But the day of the Lord will come like a thief," (2 Peter 3:10). In Revelation, Christ says, "If you are not watchful, I will come like a thief, and you will never know at what hour I will come upon you." (3:3). Other passages also emphasize the unexpected way in which Christ will return. Christ says, for example:

> "For as it was in the days of Noah, so it will be at the coming of the Son of Man. In those days before the flood, they were eating and drinking, marrying and giving in marriage, up to the day that Noah entered the ark. " (Matthew 24:37-29).

In human history, great surprises have occurred on a worldwide scale. In modern days these surprises have included the fall of the Berlin Wall and the crumbling or disintegration of the Soviet Union. But none of these surprises will ever compare with the surprise that this world will receive when Christ returns. When the heavens open and Christ appears, the world will receive the greatest impact that it has ever received. The lawyers and highest governors of world will have to interrupt their activities and recognize this event of immense magnitude. The commanders of the most powerful armies will be left completely astonished and will know that there is no way in this world to counteract the event. The communication channels will immediately abandon their ordinary programming to try to decipher and describe this event this amazing event. The officials of multi-national companies will have to put aside their monetary transactions upon realizing that something has happened that infinitely surpasses the significance of their earthly business. Those that have lived only for wealth, fame, and pleasure will have to recognize that these do not have value in comparison with the loss of their precious souls.

Let us meditate:

1. If we do not know when Christ is going to return, what should be our attitude?

2. Ignore the fact of his return because we do not know when it will be?

3. Wait until the last moment to try to prepare later?

4. Be prepared for his return, whenever it happens?
   (See 2 Peter 3:11-18.)

The Coming of Christ will be Visible

When Christ ascended into heaven, while the disciples eyes were looking up, two angels appeared, and told them, "This Jesus, who has been taken up from you into heaven will return in the same way as you have seen him going into heaven" (Acts 1:11). How did Christ ascend? He ascended in bodily form, in a visible way and in a cloud. There are several portions of Scripture that indicate that this is the form in which Christ will return. Jesus said to his disciples, "They will see the Son of Man coming in a cloud with power and great glory," (Luke 21:27).

The best way to explain the return of Christ is to describe the way in which he ascended into heaven.

1. Christ ascended in a visible form and will return in a _____ form.

2. He ascended into heaven in a bodily form and will return in a _____ form.

3. He went up into heaven in a cloud and will descend from heaven in a _____.

In all these verses we see evidence of the fact that Christ will return in a visible way, bodily form and in a cloud.

Let us meditate:

1. Why will it be necessary that Christ return in a visible and bodily form?

2. So that those who put their hope in him will have the opportunity of seeing him gloriously returning at his coming?

3. So that those that do not believe in Him are convinced that the return of Christ is Real?

4. So that his promise is fulfilled that he will return just as he left?

5. When Christ ascended into heaven, the experience was so tangible and true that the disciples were determined to give their lives as a testimony of what they had seen and experienced. When Christ returns, his coming will be so real that nobody will be able to deny the evidence.

The Return of Christ will be With Symbols of Majesty

When Christ ascended, the angels made the announcement of his return (Acts 1:11). In his second coming, Christ will come accompanied by angels (Matthew 16:27, 25:31). These divine messengers will come with Christ to render him the honor that he deserves as the Son of God. The company of angels is symbolic of majesty.

In I Thessalonians 4:16 we find a description of the majesty with which Christ will return. "For the Lord himself with a word of command, with the voice of an archangel and with the trumpet of God, will come down from heaven, and the dead in Christ will rise first." The expression "the Lord" indicates the place that Christ occupies. Paul uses the name "Jesus" to refer to the earthly ministry of our Savior. Jesus came in humiliation to give his life for us. But Paul uses the expression "Lord" to refer to the glorified Christ. He will come, as we saw in the previous verses, with great power and glory.

The expression word of command or "with a loud command" adds vigor to this authority. In the Old Testament it was used to announce a special visitation of God (see Exodus 19:16, Isaiah 27:13). In the New Testament the trumpet is used to announce transcendent events (see Matthew 24:31; Revelation 8:2-10:7). This expression also carries with it the idea of reunion. The armies used trumpets to call the soldiers and to assemble them to march to the battle. When the trumpet of God sounds, all the believers will assemble so that the Lord will carry us into heavenly places.

In his effort to describe the divine in human terms, Paul has to resort to the use of superlative vocabulary. Christ "the Lord" will return with all the symbols of power and majesty. He will come with absolute power to conclude the events of human history in accordance with his plan and his purpose.

Let us meditate:

1. He who came in humiliation will return in exaltation

2. He who came to suffer will return to reign

3. He who was judged and condemned to death will be the supreme Judge before whom the kings, the governors and all the inhabitants of the earth will bow.

What will the Coming of Christ Mean?

The coming of Christ will mean the resurrection of the dead and the rapture (transporting into heaven) of the church.

Christ Will Raise the Dead

One of the most glorious events related to the coming of Christ will be the resurrection of the dead. Paul assures us of this when he says, "For the Lord himself will come down from heaven with a loud command, with the voice of the archangel and with the trumpet call of God and the dead in Christ will rise first," (1 Thessalonians 4:16). The voice of the archangel and the sound of the trumpet will not only announce the coming of Christ, but also will penetrate the graves of those that sleep in the Lord and raise them to participate in the great celebration. "The dead in Christ" refers to those that in life had a relationship with the Lord by receiving him as their Savior. By virtue of this relationship with Christ, they will listen to the call of the Lord even from the graves. Not all of the dead will arise, only those who have believed in Him as their Savior. The Bible says, "Blessed are the dead who die in the Lord from now on," (Revelation 14:13).

Christ Will Take the Believers that are Alive

After the resurrection of the dead (in Christ), the living Christians will be taken by Christ into heaven. Paul explains, "Then we who are alive, who are left, will be caught up together with them in the clouds to meet the Lord in the air. Thus we shall always be with the Lord," (1 Thessalonians 4:17).

So the risen Christians like the living ones will be brought together in the clouds to unite with Christ. The expressions "in the air" and "in the clouds" indicate that the Christians, the living as well as the arisen, will pass from the earthly sphere to the heavenly sphere. To be with Christ is the supreme goal of every Christian. It should bring great joy to our heart knowing it is the ardent desire of our beloved Savior. He said, "Father, they are your gift to me. I wish that where I am they also may be with me, that they may see my glory that you gave me, because you loved me before the foundation of the world." (John 17:24).

Paul says to the Thessalonicans, "therefore, console one another with these words," (1 Thessalonians 4:18). These words have carried great comfort and hope to Christians in those moments of great pain when they have had to say goodbye to their loved ones at the cemetery. We have the glorious hope that, if we have already died or that if we are living, when Christ returns we will unite with Him, and will be forever with Him.

We should be aware, nevertheless, that these promises are for those that are in Christ. This refers to those that have received Christ in their heart and are living according to his will. Are we prepared for the day when Christ comes for us?

Let us meditate:

1.   Does the Bible teach that Christ will return?

2.   Does the Bible teach that all the persons are going to leave earth to live with Him?

3.   Or only those who have received him as their personal Savior?

4.   Are we prepared for his coming?

5.   Are our loved ones prepared for his coming?

6.   If they are not, what should we do?

Bible Memory Verse:

"So too, you also must be prepared, for at an hour you do not expect, the Son of Man will come." (Matthew 24:44).

Prayer:

Our Most Gracious Heavenly Father, thank you for the assurance we have that your Son Jesus is going to come back to gather those who have received him as Savior and Lord. Help me to be prepared for that day by placing all of my hope and my confidence in Jesus my Savior and not on any one else or on anything I might have done to try to merit your salvation. Help me to live the Christian life and to share it with my friends and loved ones so that they too may have the joy of going to dwell with you forever in heaven. Thank you for hearing my prayer, Amen.

Endnotes

[1] The Return of Jesus is referred to in the Mystery of the Ascension of Christ into heaven (Acts 1:11).

THE LOVING FATHER
(Luke 15:11-32)

In the previous lessons we have studied the most important events in the life of Jesus: his birth, death, resurrection, ascension, and the promise of his return. These constitute the heart of the gospel. The apostle Paul sums up the gospel when he says, "For I handed on to you as of first importance what I also received: that Christ died for our sin in accordance with the scriptures; that he was buried; that he was raised on the third day in accordance with the scriptures" (1 Corinthians 15:3-4). There is much that we can learn from these events for our spiritual benefit. What is more, there is much that we can learn from the teachings of Jesus. In this lesson we are going to focus on what Christ taught about the love of our Father who is in heaven. The Pharisees criticized Jesus because he took time to talk and eat with the publicans and the sinners. In Luke 15:11-32 we find the parable that Christ told to teach them that God is a God who loves the sinners. In this parable, the younger son represents the sinners.

In order to understand the parable better, we are going to divide it into three scenes in the life of the younger son: departure, sin, and forgiveness.

The Departure of the Prodigal Son

In verses 12 and 13 we see that the younger son asked his father for the part of the inheritance that would belong to him and he went far away to a separate province. Upon reading these words several questions come to our minds:

What Right Did He Have to Receive This Inheritance?

According to the law of the Jews of that time, the prodigal son did not have a right to receive his inheritance until his father died. The truth is that upon the passing away of the father, the inheritance was always given to the older son and later to the others. This attitude reflects the attitude that we have sometimes towards our heavenly father. He blesses us much (life, health, families, employment, intelligence, etc.), and instead of feeling grateful, we consider ourselves worthy. Paul talks about this when he asks, "Or do you hold his priceless kindness, forbearance, and patience in low esteem, unaware that the kindness of God would lead you to repentance?" (Romans 2:4; also see 1 Corinthians 4:7). All the blessings of God should convince us of his love toward us and guide us to draw near to Him.

Let us meditate:

1. What blessings have we received from God?

2. Which of these blessings do we deserve?

What is the Attitude of the Father?

The Bible says that the father divided the goods among them. The father is not happy that his son wants to leave the home, but he does not refrain him. He is going to miss him greatly; he is going to feel the separation; he is going to worry greatly for him; but he does not prevent him from going. Our heavenly Father is like this. He wants us to live in communion with Him, to be near to Him and to enjoy his blessings, but he does not force us to love him. That would not be love, but obligation.

Let us meditate:

1. God does not force us to love him. He gives us the freedom to love him or not love him, correct?

2. What is our heavenly Father like? Is he happy when we choose to live far from Him?

3. Do we show gratitude when we live lives that do not take God into account?

The Degradation of the Prodigal Son

Jesus says that the prodigal son "set off to a distant country where he squandered his inheritance on a life of dissipation" (v.13). What does it mean to be lost? (v.24). It is obvious that it does not mean that he did not know how to return.

Let us meditate:

1. In your opinion, what does it mean to be lost?

2. Does this expression refer only to those that have been "degraded themselves"?

Let us see what Christ says about those that are lost.

He was Lost Because He was Far from the Father

He was far from his father in a geographical sense. He was in a separate province. But the saddest thing is that he was far away in a spiritual sense. He did not have communication with him. He could not converse with him; he could not relate to him his worries; he could not listen to his advice.

There are people that do not believe that they are lost because they have not killed anyone or degraded themselves. But the Bible teaches that people are lost when they do not have fellowship with God. Perhaps they know that He exists and they ask him for favors when they have needs, but they have not invited him to come into their heart and to guide their life. In this sense they are lost because they do not have continual fellowship with God.

Let us meditate:

1. What are some of the ways in which we can be far from God?
    a. Rebellious activity against God? _____
    b. Indifference towards God? _____
    c. Following our own ideas? _____
    d. Simply not having time for God? _____
    e. Not knowing how to get close to God? _____

2. How close to God are we today? _____

He was Lost Because He Wasted His Resources

This passage also teaches that the prodigal son wasted his goods. Perhaps he bought luxurious clothing, acquired a mansion and threw splendid banquets in order to impress his friends. But he forgot one thing, all that he was and all that he had was received as a gift from his father. Being lost, then, was taking

173

that which his father had given him and using it in such a way that did not honor his father, violating his commands and his ideals.

In our day, being lost means taking all that God has given us - life, energy, intelligence, abilities, blessings, etc. - and using them, not to honor our heavenly Father, but rather to satisfy our own desires, to reach our own goals and to impress others. We live sinfully when we take all that God has given to us, and use it without taking him into account, as if He does not exist.

Let us meditate:

1. How are we using the resources that God has given us?
   a. Life_____
   b. Energy_____
   c. Intelligence_____
   d. Abilities_____
   e. Blessings_____

He was Lost Because He was Corrupt

Jesus says that the prodigal son, after having wasted his inheritance, began to take care of pigs (vv.14-15). For a Jew caring for pigs was the most humiliating and degrading work possible. So great was his degeneration that he desired to eat the pigs' food (v.16).

This is what sin does in the lives of people. God created us to live in communion with Him, to develop our potential and to serve humanity in his name. But the people that live far from God become victims of their own confused desires, of their vices and of the lifestyle of the persons that they are surrounded by. This at times leads them to do things that they never imagined that they would do. In other words, their life comes under the control of Satan. This brings sadness to their life, to their families that they love and to the heart of God.

Let us meditate. In the sight of God, are we living sinfully in relation to:

1. Our own desires? _____
2. Our habits? _____
3. Our lifestyle? _____
4. Our plans for our life? _____

If this were the end, this parable would be the saddest one in the Bible. But we find another scene.

The Forgiveness of the Prodigal Son

The prodigal son attained forgiveness for two reasons. One was what he did to draw near to God. The other was what God did in order to receive him. Let us look at these two parts.

What the Prodigal Son Did

Jesus teaches that the prodigal son did not remain in his degenerated condition. He did several things that led him to receive the forgiveness of his father.

The Prodigal Son Reflected

The prodigal son reflected, and "coming to his senses he thought, How many of my father's hired workers have more than enough food to eat, but here am I, dying from hunger" (v.17). The expression "coming to his senses" is very descriptive. Before, he was beside of himself, he was not thinking in a reasonable way. He was not himself. He reflected, made an analysis of his life, and recognized his situation.

It is a very significant day when people come to their senses, when they examine their life in the light of the Word of God and realize that this is not the kind of life that He wants them to live. God does not want them to live chained by their passions, imprisoned by their whims, and impoverished by their bad decisions. God wants to give them a life full of blessings. Christ said, "I came so that they might have life and have it more abundantly" (John 10:10).

Let us meditate. Will this be the moment in which we reflect and ask ourselves:

1. Is this the kind of life that God wants me to live, or is there a better life for me?

2. Is my life going in the right direction, or do I feel that my life is out of control?

3. Am I bringing happiness or sadness to my loved ones with the kind of life that I am living?

The Prodigal Son Repented

> "I shall get up and go to my father and I shall say to
> him, "Father, I have sinned against heaven and against you.
> I no longer deserve to be called your son; treat me as you
> would treat one of your hired workers" (vv.18-19).

The prodigal son recognized his sin and decided to ask for forgiveness from his father. Repentance is necessary for forgiveness. Repentance means that we feel burdened by our sin, that we are willing to confess it and to make the decision to separate ourselves from it. This was the first message of Jesus Christ, "repent, and believe in the gospel" (Mark 1:15).

Let us meditate:

1.   Do I feel burdened by my sins?

2.   Am I willing to confess my sins to God?

3.   Am I willing to separate myself from them?

The Prodigal Son Returned to the Father

"So he got up and went back to his father" (v.20). The prodigal son not only reflected, not only repented, but also returned to his father. He got up from the pigpen and made his way toward his father. This means that he was willing to abandon his lifestyle, to leave behind his supposed friends who had only carried him into perdition, and to begin to live the kind of life that would honor his father.

There are many people who feel remorse for the sins that they have committed, who feel guilt for the type of life that they are living, or who at least feel troubled because they know that their life is not honoring God, but they continue in this manner. They do not draw near to God. The prodigal son would not have received forgiveness if he had not returned to the father.

Let us meditate:

1. Am I willing to return to my heavenly Father?

2. Am I ready to receive his love and his forgiveness?

3. Am I willing to live close to Him?

What the Father Did

The Father Responded to His Son

> "So he got up and went back to his father. While he was still a long way off, his father caught sight of him, and was filled with compassion. He ran to his son, embraced him and kissed him" (v.20).

The Father Received His Son

This verse says several important things about the father.

In the first place, he was waiting for his son. Each day he went out to look toward the horizon, longing for his son to return. This reflects the attitude of our heavenly Father. The apostle Peter says that God waits with patience, not wanting anyone to perish but for all to come to repentance" (2 Peter 3:9).

In the second place, the father was moved to mercy. When he saw his son, instead of feeling bitterness or anger for what his son had done, he felt compassion. This also reveals to us the character of our Heavenly Father. His Word says, "Merciful and gracious is the Lord, slow to anger, abounding in kindness" (Psalm 103:8). The Word of God says that Jesus was moved to compassion upon seeing the multitudes that were as sheep without a shepherd (Mark 6:34). We can have the assurance that if we draw near to God with repentant hearts, He will have mercy on us, and forgive us no matter what has been our sin.

In the third place, the father kissed his son. This tells us clearly about the love that he had towards his son. Jesus speaks of the love of God when he says, "for God so loved the world that he gave his only son, so that everyone who believes in him might not perish but might have eternal life" (John 3:16).

Let us meditate:

1. What concept do we have of our heavenly Father?

2. A vindictive God or a compassionate God?

3. What does it mean for me to know that God is waiting for me to draw near to Him?

4. What does it mean for me to know that God is ready to show us his love?

The Father Restored His Son

The prodigal son would have been comfortable with being a servant in his father's house (v.19), but the father restored him as a son.

> "But his father ordered his servants, 'Quickly bring the finest robe and put it on him; put a ring on his finger and sandals on his feet. Take the fattened calf and slaughter it. Then let us celebrate with a feast, because this son of mine was dead, and has come to life again; he was lost, and has been found'" (vv.22-24).

The robe, the ring and the calf, all indicated that the prodigal was a son with all the privileges in his father's house. Jesus expresses this same idea when he says, "But to those who did accept him he gave power to become children of God, to those who believe in his name" (John 1:12).

Let us meditate:

1. In view of such a clear manifestation of the love of God towards us, the question that each one should ask is 'have I received Christ as my personal savior?

Bible Memory Verse:

> "But to those who did accept him, he gave power to become children of God, to those who believe in his name" (John 1:12).

Prayer:

Dear Heavenly Father, like the Prodigal Son, I recognize the fact that I have strayed from you, violated your commandments, and broken your heart. I repent of my sins and ask you to forgive me and to accept me as your child. Thank you for loving me and for hearing my prayer. Amen.

THE NEW BIRTH
(John 3:1-16)

In addition to giving divine teachings about the love of God, Jesus taught about the change that this love produces in a person's life. In John chapter 3 we find that Jesus taught a man named Nicodemus about this subject.

Upon reading this chapter we realize that Nicodemus was an outstanding person.

First, he was very intelligent. He said to Jesus, "we know that you are a teacher who has come from God, for no one can do these signs that you are doing unless God is with him" (v. 2). Even though others from the Pharisees did not want to accept the fact that Jesus was the Son of God, Nicodemus considered carefully the miracles of Jesus and came to the conclusion that he had come from God.

Second, Nicodemus was very religious. He was a leader, "a ruler of the Jews" (v. 1). He belonged to the Sanhedrin, which was the supreme court of the Jews. The Sanhedrin had authority over all the Jewish religious matter for the entire world.

Third, Nicodemus was a very cautious man. He "came to Jesus by night" (v. 2). He came at an hour when he could talk with Jesus alone and consider carefully what He had to say about the Kingdom of God.

Fourth, Nicodemus was rich. In John 19:39 we read that Nicodemus brought 100 pounds of a mixture of myrrh and aloes to prepare Jesus' body for the tomb. Only a rich person could buy such a great quantity of myrrh and aloes.

One of the most surprising things about Jesus and Nicodemus' conversation is that he told him he had to be born again (John 3:3). It would be very easy to understand if Jesus had said that to a degenerate and perverse person. But Nicodemus was intelligent, religious, cautious, and apparently blessed with material wealth.

Let us meditate:

1. Can a person be intelligent, religious, prudent, and rich and still have emptiness in his life?

2. What surprises us most is that Nicodemus was religious but was still looking for something that would fill his soul. Is there a difference between simply following religious practices and having a personal relationship with Christ?

3. What did Jesus teach him about the new birth and what does this mean for our life?

Jesus Taught that the New Birth is Necessary

In spite of being very religious, Nicodemus had to understand the new birth.

It is More than having a Lofty Concept About Jesus

Nicodemus knew that Jesus was a teacher, but this was not sufficient. Nicodemus had to accept him as his personal Savior. John says, "But to those who did accept him he gave power to become children of God, to those who believe in his name" (1:12). Nicodemus believed in the miracles that Jesus had done, but he had to experience the miracle of miracles. The complete change that Christ could make in a person's life. He had seen signs of the Kingdom of God, but he had not been able to see the Kingdom fully nor enter into it without this radical change in his life. It is not sufficient to know that Jesus is a teacher, that he can do miracles and that he has the evidence of the Kingdom of God in his ministry. One must completely present or surrender one's life to Jesus in order for God to produce a change so great and so glorious that we have to call it a new birth.

Let us meditate:

1. Has there been a moment in my life in when I have invited Christ to come into my heart?

2. Has Christ changed my life in such a way that I am a new person?

It is More than a Change that the Person has Made in His Life

The word that Jesus uses to explain the new birth indicates that this is not something that the person can do for himself. Being born again is being born from above. Let us study the meaning of this more closely. Being born from above means that it is something that only God can do. It is not a natural birth but rather a supernatural one. Only God can change the life of a person to such a degree that he is truly a new person. When Christ died, he did for us that which we could not do for ourselves. Through the ages man has tried to reform his life, only to conclude that his effort is useless. When we invite Christ, he enters into our life, cleanses us of our sin, and changes our attitudes, our thoughts, our impulses, and our desires. Paul explains this when he says, "So whoever is in Christ is a new creation: old things have passed away; behold, new things have come" (2 Corinthians 5:17). The new birth is something that only God can do.

Let us meditate:

1. Have I tried to change my life by my own strength?

2. What has been the result?

3. Am I willing to recognize that only God can change my life radically?

Jesus Taught Us that the New Birth is Spiritual

At first Nicodemus did not understand what Jesus was saying. He asked him: "How can a person once grown old be born again? Surely he cannot reenter his mother's womb and be born again, can he?" (John 3:4).

A Spiritual Birth

Jesus explained to Nicodemus that the new life is not a physical birth. He told him, "I say to you, no one can enter the Kingdom of God without being born of water and Spirit" (v. 5). Nicodemus was thinking in physical terms, but Jesus helped him see that He was speaking in spiritual terms. "What is born of flesh is flesh and what is born of spirit is spirit" (v. 6). Physically, if Nicodemus could have been born a hundred times, he would still be the same person, because in each case, he would have the same tendencies toward sin and evil. Nicodemus needed a change in his spirit, his true

183

personality. The spirit of Nicodemus had to change in such a way that he would be as a born again person, innocent, pure, clean, and free from the slavery and stain of sin.

Let us meditate:

1.   Many of the changes that we experience are superficial, external and temporary. Are we able to name any of these?

2.   The spiritual change of which Christ speaks is internal and lasting. Are we willing to permit Christ to renew our soul, our mind, and our personality?

3.   This is what "being born of the spirit" means. Have we been born again spiritually?

A Birth Through the Spirit

Without doubt Nicodemus, who depended on his ability to keep all the laws of the Jewish religion, felt unable to change his life completely in order to please God. Jesus helped him see that this birth does not happen through the strength of individual will, but rather through the work of the Holy Spirit. Jesus explained to him, "The wind blows where it wills, and you can hear the sound it makes, but you do not know where it comes from or where it goes; so it is with everyone who is born of the Spirit" (v. 8). We cannot see the wind, but we are able to feel its effect. No one who has felt a tornado, a hurricane, or simply a strong wind can deny the existence of the wind. Although we do not see it, we are familiar with its effect. So is the work of the Holy Spirit in our hearts. We cannot see it, but we do know its effect, demolishing the barriers that separate us from God, breaking the chains that enslave us, sweeping away the sin that stains our life, and giving us that divine gust of the presence of God in our heart.

Let us meditate:

1.   The Spirit of God has the power to forgive all our sins and to change our life completely. Do we believe that God can do this in our life?

2.   Are we willing to put our faith in Jesus Christ in order to change our life through his Spirit?

184

Jesus Explained that the New Birth is Made Possible Through His Death on the Cross

Even after Jesus explain the nature of the new birth to him; Nicodemus did not understand how such a radical change would be possible. In order to help him to understand this, Jesus utilized something that Nicodemus understood well. He told him, "And just as Moses lifted up the serpent in the wilderness, so the Son of Man must be lifted up" (v. 14).

The Example of the Serpent in the Wilderness

Nicodemus recalled the story to which Jesus referred. When the people of Israel had rebelled against God and were dying as a result of snakebites, God commanded Moses to make a serpent of bronze and to raise it. All those that put their faith in Him and accepted his provision were saved from sure death (Numbers 21:4-9). The Jewish people had to understand that only by faith in that which God had done for them could they be saved from death.

The Effectiveness of the Cross of Calvary

With this example in the history of the Jewish people, Jesus explained to Nicodemus that He was going to be raised on a cross in order that all those who through faith accepted his sacrifice were saved from their sins and from eternal death. Paul explained this when he said, "But God proves his love for us in that while we were still sinners Christ died for us" (Romans 5:8). He also writes:

> "And you who were once alienated and hostile in mind because of evil deeds he has now reconciled in his fleshly body through his death, to present you holy, without blemish, and irreproachable before him." (Colossians 1:21-22).

It is very important that we recognize that the new birth is not something that we are able to attain through human effort, but, only through that which Christ did for us by dying on the cross.

Let us mediate:

1.   The Jewish people by faith saw the remedy that God provided and received his healing. Those that did not believe in the remedy died in their rebellion and their incredulity.

2.   The death of Jesus on the cross is the remedy that God has provided for our eternal salvation. If we believe in Him as our Savior, we receive the remedy of God.

3.   If we refuse to believe in Christ as our personal Savior, will we find another remedy in the Bible? Read John 3:18.

Jesus taught us that the new birth is necessary in order to enter into heaven.

The Necessity of the New Birth

Even though Nicodemus understood much about the religious laws of the Jews and was strengthened by keeping them, he did not have any idea of the importance of the new birth. Jesus helped him to see that the new birth was absolutely necessary in order to enter into heaven. Jesus told him, "I say to you, no one can see the Kingdom of God without being born from above" (v. 3). Later he repeated, "I say to you no one can enter the Kingdom of God without being born of water and Spirit" (v. 5). It is important that we understand that Jesus is not saying that we need to have a certain amount of knowledge, that we have to attend church a certain number of times, or do charitable works, or to give a certain amount of money to enter into the Kingdom of God. Although all these things are good and can be evidence of that which is in our heart, Jesus said: "No one can see the Kingdom of God without being born from above."

Let us meditate:

1.   What is it that Christ says is necessary to enter into heaven?

   a.   To have a certain amount of knowledge?

   b.   To attend church a certain number of times?

   c.   To do charitable acts?

d. To give to a certain amount of money?

e. To be born again?

f. In light of this, it is important that I ask myself, have I been born again?

The Way in which the New Birth is Received

If the new birth is necessary in order for us to enter into heaven, should we ask ourselves, 'What do I need to do to experience the new birth?' Jesus answered this question when he said to Nicodemus, "For God so loved the world that he gave his only Son, so that everyone who believes in him might not perish but might have eternal life" (3:16). It is very clear that we need to believe in Christ as our Savior. But to believe in Him means more than simply to know that he exists, that he is the Son of God, or that he died on the cross.

Let us meditate:

To believe in Him means putting our confidence in Him in such a way that we invite him into our heart so that he comes to:

1. Wash us of our sins

2. Remove all our feelings of guilt

3. Change the direction of our life

4. Purify our desires, ambitions and passions

5. Give us a new position, a new hope and profound assurance that when we die we will go to be with him.

Let us review this list and mark those characteristics that are present in our life.

1. I have believed in Jesus Christ:
   a. That He is the Son of God.
   b. That He died on the cross for my sins
   c. That he rose from the dead.

2. I have put all my confidence in Him.
   a. I have received Him as my Savior.

The change that Christ makes in our life is so marvelous, so complete and so glorious that the only way in which we can describe it is to say that we have been born again.

Bible Memory Verse:

"I say to you, no one can see the Kingdom of God without being born from above." (John 3:3)

Prayer:

Dear Jesus, Thank you for coming to earth to give your life so that we can have a new life in you. I place my complete trust in you as my Savior and pray that I will experience the new birth that is made possible through faith in you. Thank you for hearing my prayer. Amen.

THE PROPER RELATIONSHIP WITH GOD
(John 4:1-26)

During his ministry, Jesus not only taught about the love God and the new birth, but he also spoke about what true worship is.

One of the people with whom Christ spoke about true worship was the Samaritan woman (John 4:4-6). She came to draw water from the well that Jacob, one of the patriarchs of the Jewish people, had dug. Jesus, who was tired from the journey, said to her, "Give me a drink" (v. 7). This surprised the Samaritan woman "for Jews use nothing in common with Samaritans" (v. 9). With his actions, Jesus demonstrated to her that the love of God extends toward all persons, and with his words he showed her worship that does not honor God, and the worship that does honor God.

The Worship that God Does Not Desire

The Samaritans were a blending of Jewish and Gentile people groups. When the people of Israel were carried as captive to Babylon, a small number of Jews stayed in Israel. "The king of Assyria brought people from Babylon, Cuthah, Avva, Hamath, and Sepharvaim and settled them in the cities of Samaria in place of the Israelites" (2 Kings 17:24). With the passing of time, Jews that stayed in Samaria became mixed in marriage with the Gentiles that had come from the different nations. The Jews, upon marrying people who were not Jews, not only mixed their cultures but also their religions. This was evident in the worship of the Samaritans. The Bible explains, "But these peoples began to make their own gods in the various cities in which they were living; in the shrines on the high places which the Samaritans had made, each people set up gods" (2 Kings 17:29). So that Samaritans were practicing a mix of Judaism and paganism in their worship. For this reason, Christ pointed out to the Samaritan woman the kind of worship that does not honor God.

God Does Not Desire Selective Worship

The worship that does not honor God chooses only that which it wishes about Him and does not pay attention to the other important things that he has revealed in his Word. For example, the Samaritans decided to accept only the first five books of the Bible. Although these five books (Genesis, Exodus, Leviticus, Numbers and Deuteronomy) are very valuable, they do not represent the complete revelation of God. Therefore by leaving out the other books of the Old Testament, the Samaritans missed many things that God wanted them to know in order that they might render to him the worship that honors him. In the other books of the Old Testament, for example, God reveals much about his character, his love, his providence, his patience, his justice, and his promise to send his Son, Jesus Christ. These books also contain important teachings about true worship in contrast to the worship of the pagan gods.

He who practices selective worship does not please God because he does not take into account his complete revelation, but instead chooses only that which is convenient for him and which he wishes to believe. There are people that only use the parts of the Bible that please them, without paying attention to the parts that speak about the way in which God should be worshipped and the type of life that people that worship God should live. For example, there are people that only concentrate on the announcement of the birth of Jesus in their worship. Although this is a very important part in the Word of God, there is much more of the life of Jesus that one should take into account. There are other people that only focus their attention on the death of Jesus in their worship. This also is an important aspect of the gospel, because without it there would have been no salvation for humanity. But, on focusing all our devotion only on the crucified Christ, we are leaving out an important part of his mission. The Bible teaches that Christ was not permanently on the cross. He rose, ascended into heaven, seated himself at the right hand of God (where he intercedes for us) and, through his Spirit, lives in our heart if we have accepted him as Savior. Worship that focuses only on some aspects of the life of Jesus and leaves out others does not please God. He wants us to receive all the blessing that he desires to give us through his Son Jesus.

Let's meditate:

1. Are we practicing selective worship, concentrating only on:

   a. The announcement of the birth of Jesus in such a way that we are concentrating on the messenger and not on the message about the Savior of the world?

   b. The birth of Jesus in such a way that we think of Jesus only as a baby?

    c.   The crucified Christ in such a way that we do not think of the resurrected Christ?

    d.   The buried Christ in such a way that we do not think of the resurrected Christ, who arose into heaven and is at the right hand of God, interceding for us?

2.   The worship that pleases God takes into account the complete gospel of the announcement, the birth, the teachings, the death, the resurrection, the ascension, the intercession and the second coming of Jesus Christ.

God Does Not Desire Worship Based on Ignorance

Jesus told the Samaritan woman, "You people worship what you do not understand" (John 4:22). She had asked where she should worship, on the mount of Jerusalem or on the mount of Samaria (Gerezim). At first sight it seems that one place is good as the other. But the truth is that those who were worshipping on Gerezim did not have a clear concept of the nature of God and the instructions that he had given about how one should worship him. This woman was only following the tradition of her parents, who had decided to worship on their own mount for political reasons. The king of the kingdom to the north (where Samaria was) had built his own altars in Gerezim in order that the people would not go out of the kingdom to the south (where Jerusalem was) to worship. The Word of God says:

> "They did not listen, however, but continued in their earlier manner. Thus these nations venerated the LORD, but also served their idols. And their sons and grandsons, to this day, are doing as their fathers did" (2 Kings 17:40-41).

What Jesus is telling the Samaritan woman is that she does not really know God, but that she is simply following the traditions of her ancestors by worshipping on that mount. Worship based on ignorance does not please God because it does not take into account what He has revealed about his character.

Let us meditate:

1. It is good to have respect and to show appreciation toward our ancestors, but does God want us to study his Holy Word for ourselves so that we might know how we should worship him?

2. What does Christ's expression mean that we should worship God "in Spirit and truth" (John 4:24)?

   a. "In Spirit" is with an open and sincere heart. Am I worshipping him like that?

   b. "In truth" is with the knowledge of the Word of God. Am I making an effort to study the Bible?

God Does Not Desire Syncretistic (Mixed) Worship

The worship that had been established on Gerezim was a mixture of Judaism and paganism. The Bible explains that they worshipped the Lord, but "they served their own gods, following the worship of the nations from among whom they had been deported" (2 Kings 17:33). They had adopted all types of pagan practices in their worship. They did not stop worshipping God, but simply added beliefs and practices – such as burning their children as sacrifices. In this passage and in many others it is obvious that this does not please God. Verses 35 and 36 make this very clear when they say:

> "You must not venerate other gods, nor worship them, nor serve them, nor offer sacrifice to them. The LORD, who brought you up from the land of Egypt with great power and outstretched arm: Him shall you venerate, Him shall you worship, and to Him shall you sacrifice."

Let us meditate:

1. Some persons were great examples for humanity and we should honor them, but be should we worship them?

2. In light of these passages who is the one that deserves all our worship?

God Does Not Desire Superstitious Worship

The passage of 2 Kings 127:16-17 describes the worship of the Samaritans:

> "They disregarded all the commandments of the LORD, their God, and made for themselves two molten calves; they also made a sacred pole and worshipped all the host of heaven, and served Baal. They immolated their sons and daughters by fire, practiced fortune-telling and evildoing in the LORD's sight, provoking him."

As we can see, this worship included divination, witchcraft, astrology, and human sacrifices. There is a huge difference in worship based on superstition and true worship. True worship seeks and submits itself to the will of God. Christ gave us the example when he prayed before dying on the cross: "not my will, but yours be done" (Luke 22:42). He taught us to pray: "Your will be done, on earth as it is in heaven" (Matthew 6:10). Worship based on superstition tries to force God (or the spirits) to do the will of the person that is asking. Through formulas, rites, ceremonies, or canticles, the person tries to get what he wants, whether it is good or bad. When the Samaritans practiced these types of witchcraft, divination, astrology, and sacrifices, they did evil before the eyes of Jehovah and provoked his anger (v. 17). God became so angry with them that he removed them from his presence (v. 18). The attitude of God is the same today towards those that practice witchcraft and other forms of superstitious worship. God will judge these people.

Let us mediate:

1. Can our worship be a mixture of Christianity and paganism?

2. Just like the Samaritans that "feared God" and at the same time served idols, are we mixing our worship?

3. Are we truly basing worship on what the Word of God teaches us?

4. Is God pleased if we consult diviners, healers, astrologers, and witches?

The Worship that God Does Desire

Worship that Proceeds from a Correct Relationship with God

While speaking with the Samaritan woman, Jesus explained to her that the worship that God desires is one that proceeds from a correct relationship with God. Christ told her, "If you knew the gift of God and who it is saying to you, 'Give me a drink," you would have asked him and he would have given you living water" (John 4:10). The "gift of God" refers to the gift that God has given to humanity. Christ explained to Nicodemus, "For God so loved the world that he gave his only Son, so that everyone who believes in him might no perish but might have eternal life" (John 3:16). If we receive this gift of God, we have salvation (eternal life).

In his conversation with the Samaritan woman, Christ compared salvation with living water. He told her, "whoever drinks the water I shall give will never thirst; the water I shall give will become in him a spring of water welling up to eternal life" (v. 14). Christ was not speaking of physical water, but rather of his spiritual presence in the heart of those that receive him. The presence of Christ in the heart satisfies our spiritual thirst. Saint Augustine said, 'You have created us for yourself and our hearts are restless until we find rest in you." The presence of Christ satisfies so that we do not need anything else to satisfy the thirst of our soul. His presence produces such happiness that is like a fountain that is overflowing and never runs dry. This is the salvation that Christ gives to those who receive him, it assures people of eternal life with Him in heaven.

I order to receive this salvation; the person needs to believe in Christ as his personal Savior. It took time for the Samaritan woman to understand who Jesus was and to put her confidence in Him. Upon reading the whole passage, we see that she first referred to Him as:

1. A Jew (a stranger, v. 9).

2. Later as sir (a respected person, v. 11); later as a prophet (a religious man sent by God, v. 19).

3. Finally she recognized that Jesus was the Messiah (the Christ, the Savior of the world, vv. 25, 29).

We need to ask ourselves: Who is Jesus for me? In order that we might have salvation and worship God, as He desires, it is necessary that individually we receive Christ as our personal Savior.

Let us meditate: What concept do I have of Jesus Christ?

1. A stranger that I do not know personally?

2. A good man whom I respect?

3. A messenger sent by God?

4. My personal Savior whom I have invited into my heart?

Worship that is Offered in a Spiritual Way

The woman was asking Christ where she should worship. Christ answered her by saying that the most important thing was not where but how.

> "Jesus said to her, Believe me, woman, the hour is coming when you will worship the Father neither on this mountain nor in Jerusalem. But the hour is coming, and is now here, when true worshippers will worship the Father in Spirit and truth; and indeed the Father seeks such people to worship him. God is Spirit and those who worship mush worship in Spirit and truth" (vv. 21, 23-24).

The expression "God is Spirit," means that one cannot capture him in a place or in a physical object. That which we offer him in worship should not be material things, but rather spiritual gifts, such as love, loyalty, obedience, and devotion. As a spiritual being, God requires spiritual worship.

Let us meditate:

1. Because God desires spiritual worship, should we focus our attention on material objects or on God himself?

2. If Christ does not dwell in our heart, are we able to worship God in spirit and in truth?

3.   Has the presence of Christ satisfied the thirst of my heart?

4.   The worship that God desires, therefore, it is not selective, ignorant, syncretic (mixed), nor superstitious, but worship that proceeds from a correct relationship with Him and is offered in a spiritual way. Are we worshipping God in this way?

Bible Memory Verse:

"God is Sprit and those who worship him must worship in Spirit and truth" (John 4:24).

Prayer:

Dear Jesus, thank you for teaching us how to worship God. Please help me to know how to worship Him in spirit and truth. Amen.

THE FINAL DESTINY
(Luke 16:19-31)

One of the most important teachings of Jesus has to do with the final destiny of people. In order to illustrate what he wanted people to understand Jesus told the parable of the rich man Lazarus (Luke 16:19-31). For a moment in this parable the curtain of eternity is lifted and we are able to see what happens after death. Upon reading this parable some are happy to know Lazarus, who experienced pain, sickness, loneliness, and hunger, finally knows what it is to be in the presence of God, where the tears are wiped away and burdens are lifted. On the other hand, some are happy to know that the rich man, who was surrounded by luxury, fame and comfort, in the end knows what it is like to be thirsty and endure anguish. But the purpose of this parable is not to teach that the rich are condemned and the poor are saved. There are deep and valuable truths in this parable of our Lord Jesus Christ.

There is Life After Death

Through this parable Jesus taught that the life of a human being does not end when one dies.

Lazarus Died and was Raised by Angels into Heaven

Jesus clearly says that the spirit of Lazarus continued living when he died physically (v. 22). In this verse the expression "to the bosom of Abraham" means Abraham's side. The Jews used this expression to mean heaven, the place of blessing. To be at the side of Abraham means that Lazarus was received enthusiastically by the father of the people of God. Upon ending his existence here upon earth, the spirit of Lazarus was carried by the angels into heaven.

Let us meditate:

1. What evidence do we have from this parable that the Word of God teaches that there is life after death?

2. What evidence do we have in this parable that the Word of God teaches that the soul, the center of our personality, continues living after physical death?

3. Where does the Bible say that the spirit of Lazarus was carried?

Verse 22 says, "the rich man also died and was buried." It would have been one of the most important and most luxurious funerals of the town. But the funeral of the rich man did not mark the end of his existence. The 23rd verse says that in hell "from the netherworld, where he was in torment, he raised his eyes and saw Abraham far off and Lazarus at his side." The fact that it is a place of suffering is seen in the description of the rich man that he was "in torment."

In other parts of the Scriptures, Jesus spoke clearly about the two places where people go when they die. In Matthew 25:46, he said, "these will go off to eternal punishment, but the righteous to eternal life." In Matthew 23, Jesus condemned the hypocrisy of the Pharisees and told them, "You serpents, you brood of vipers, how can you flee from the judgment of Gehenna?" (Hell) (v. 33). On the other hand, Jesus explained that He descended from heaven (John 3:13) and said to them that there is joy in heaven when a sinner repents (Luke 15:7). Lazarus died and was raised by the angels into heaven. The rich man died and opened his eyes in the place of torment. Jesus taught that those that died go to one of two place, heaven or hell.

Let us meditate:

1. Jesus said that the rich man died and was buried. Was this the end of the   rich man's existence?

2. Where does the Word of God say that the rich man opened his eyes?

3. Upon reading this parable of the Lord Jesus Christ, can we conclude that all people go to the same place when they die?

4. Does the Bible clearly teach that there is a place of torment and a place of blessing?

5. That we decide our future while we are alive?

Jesus taught that while they are alive, people determine where they are going to spend eternity. We see this in the request of the rich man and the answer of Abraham.

The Request of the Rich Man

"And he cried out, 'Father Abraham, have pity on me. Send Lazarus to dip the tip of his finger in water and cool my tongue, for I am suffering torment in these flames.'" (v. 24). He who never had mercy on the beggar Lazarus now was asking for mercy. The 19th verse says that the rich man "dined sumptuously each day." But in the midst of his luxury and his abundance, he did not pay attention to the beggar that was at his door "covered with sores" (v. 20) and hungered, even "would gladly have eaten his fill of the scraps that fell from the rich man's table" (v. 21).

It is clear that the rich man was not condemned because he was rich, but rather because he did not take God into account in his life. This is reflected in the way in which he turned his back on the poor beggar.

On the other hand, Lazarus was not saved because he was poor. The name, Lazarus, means, "God is my helper." Although Lazarus did not have material goods, nor did he have enough food, he had placed his confidence in God. Because of this he enjoyed the blessing of heaven.

The rich man experienced torment, and asked that Lazarus come to ease his thirst. So great was his torment that only a drop of water might bring him relief.

Let us meditate:

1. What evidence do we have in this parable that the rich man did not take God into account during his life?

2. What evidence do we have that the rich man was looking for relief for his situation?

CHAPTER 23

The Answer Given by Abraham

Abraham answered him, "between us and you a great chasm has been established to prevent anyone from crossing who might wish to go from our side to yours or from your side to ours" (v. 26). Through this word, Jesus taught that the final destiny of people is permanent. He said to Nicodemus, for example, that those that put their confidence in Him have "eternal life" (John 3:16). Life in heaven with Jesus is not temporary. It is for all eternity. Jesus taught the same thing about condemnation in hell. We note what he said, "If your hand or you foot causes you to sin, cut it off and throw it away. It is better for you to enter into life maimed or crippled than with two hands or two feet to be thrown into eternal fire" (Matthew 18:8). Jesus talked about eternal life and eternal death. Eternal life refers to heaven, while eternal death refers to hell. If both are eternal, they cannot be only for a time.

There are people that think that the punishment is too severe. Jesus knew that the punishment was so severe that He was willing to give his life on the cross in order to free us from condemnation. That is why he says, "I say to you, whoever hears my word and believes in the one who sent me has eternal life and will not come to condemnation, but has passed from death to life" (John 5:24). It is true that the condemnation is forever, but it is also true that the salvation that Christ offers us is eternal. Jesus taught that those who die are going to one of two places, heaven or hell. He taught us that those that arrive in those places are going to be there forever. Along with this frightening message about condemnation, Jesus gave the glorious message of salvation. People make their own decision about their final destiny in this life. Jesus said, "Whoever believes in the Son has eternal life, but whoever disobeys (rejects) the Son will not see life, but the wrath of God remains on him" (John 3:36).

Let us meditate:

1. Was the rich man's request that Lazarus come to where he was, granted?

2. Does this parable indicate that people can go from hell to heaven?

3. Did Abraham say that there was a place between heaven and hell (v. 26)?

4. When Abraham said to him, "My child remember" (v. 25), is he reminding the rich man that he had opportunities to take God into account during his life?

5. What should we do with the opportunities that God gives us to take him into account during our lives?

6. In light of this parable, does it make sense for us to wait until the last hour to draw close to God?

The Way We Respond to the Gospel Determines Where We Will Spend Eternity

The Request of the Rich Man

Upon realizing that his condition in hell was permanent, the rich man began to worry about his brothers. He says to Abraham, "Then I beg you father, send him to my father's house, for I have five brothers, so that he may warn them, lest they too come to this place of torment" (vv. 27-28). The rich man knows that he cannot do anything about his own condition. He wasted the opportunities when he lived here on the earth. But he did not want his brothers to commit the same fatal mistake. Because of this he wanted someone to go and witness to them so that they would not come to the same place.

Abraham's Answer

Abraham answered him: "They have Moses and the prophets. Let them listen to them" (v. 29). The way in which the Jews used the name of Moses meant that the law of God had been given to Moses. "The Prophets" referred to the preachers. Abraham was saying, "they have the Word of God and they have the preachers. If they do not want to go to hell, they might hear the Word of God and listen to the message of God through the prophets."

The rich man did not believe this was enough and because of this he suggested, "Oh no, father Abraham, but if someone from the dead goes to them, they will repent" (v. 30). The rich man believed that if someone returned from the grave and preached to them, surely they are going to repent.

Abraham answered him, "If they will not listen to Moses and the prophets, neither will they be persuaded if someone should rise from the dead" (v. 31). If people close their hearts to the message of the messengers of God, they are not going to receive the message of someone that comes from the grave and preaches to them.

201

We find an example of this in the way in which the Pharisees reacted when Jesus raised Lazarus from the dead. This should have been the miracle that convinced them that Jesus truly was the Son of God. But instead of believing, they shut their hearts and tried to murder, not only Lazurus, but also Jesus (John 12:9-11). And the worst thing is that many kept their hearts closed after the resurrection. If they have closed their hearts, nothing is going to convince them that they should repent of their sin, receive Christ into their heart and live for Him, not only avoiding the eternal punishment but also receiving the great blessing of eternal life with Him.

What Abraham said is a significant truth for us in our day. Today we have the faithful and worthy testimony of the Word of God. We also have the servants of God that faithfully teach his Word. The Word of God teaches that Jesus Christ is the only way that God has provided the salvation of humanity.

Let us consider what Paul says:

> "For everyone who calls on the name of Lord will be saved. But how can they call on him in whom they have not believed? And how can they believe in him of whom they have not heard? And how can they hear without someone to preach? And how can people preach unless they are sent? As it is written, 'how beautiful are the feet of those who bring the good news!'" (Romans 10:13-15)

The plan that God has for people that are going to heaven instead of the place of torment is that they need to listen to the gospel (the good news) and receive Jesus Christ as the Lord of their life. What then is the gospel? It is the good news that God sent his Son, Jesus Christ, to do that which man could not do for himself – free himself from the consequences of his sin. Paul explains this when he says, "For the wages of sin death, but the gift of God is eternal life in Christ Jesus our Lord" (Romans 6:23). God sent Christ to die for us, and when we receive him as our Lord we receive eternal life. Jesus said, "Whoever believes in the Son has eternal life, but whoever disobeys (rejects) the Son will not see life, for God's wrath remains on him" (John 3:36).

Let us meditate:

In this life we have testimony of the Word of God. In it we find all the instruction necessary to recieve salvation. Read 2 Timothy 3:15.

1. Are we willing to trust in the Word of God as the supreme authority that teaches us how to receive our salvation?

2. What should we do in order to understand what the Word of God says about our salvation?

3. Should we read it daily?

4. Should we study it sincerely?

5. Should we accept what it says?

6. Should we believe in other sources of information more than in the Word of God?

7. The expression, "the Prophets" refers to those that preach the Word of God. What does Abraham say that we should do in response to the prophets?

8. The rich man was worried for his brothers when it was too late.

   a. Should we worry about whether our loved ones receive Christ in their hearts?

   b. What are we doing in order that they might know Christ as their personal Savior?

Through this parable Jesus taught that:

1. There is life after death – Are we convinced of this?

2. While we are still living we decide where we are going to spend eternity – Have we made the decision of receiving Christ?

3. We will spend eternity in heaven or in hell – Are we sure of where we are going?

4. The way in which we respond to the gospel determines our final destiny – How have we responded to the message of Jesus Christ?

Because this is such an important matter, the Word of God says, "in an acceptable time I heard you, and on the day of salvation I helped you. Behold.

now is a very acceptable time; behold, now is the day of salvation" (2 Corinthians 6:2). "Therefore, as the Holy Spirit says: 'Oh, that today you would hear his voice, Harden not your hearts as at the rebellion in the day of testing in the desert'" (Hebrews 3:7-8).

Bible Memory Verse:

"Whoever believes in the Son has eternal life, but whoever disobeys (rejects) the Son will not see life, but the wrath of God remains upon him" (John 3:36).

Prayer:

Our most Gracious Heavenly Father, I want to be completely sure that I am going to be with you when I die. I know that on my own merit I am not worthy to go to heaven. I thank you that you sent Jesus to die in my place. While I am alive and have an opportunity, I want to place my complete trust in Jesus as my Savior. Thank you for the assurance I have that you have prepared a place for me in heaven. Amen.

CONCLUSION

The purpose of this book, *The Gospel in the Rosary: Bible Study on the Mysteries of Christ*, is "to bring out fully the Christological depth of the Rosary"[1] in order to encourage people to have a personal and living relationship with Jesus Christ.

In his Apostolic Letter, Pope John Paul II, expressed concern that the Rosary not become merely a mechanical exercise. He explained:

> In effect, the Rosary is simply a *method of contemplation*. As a method, it serves as a means to an end and cannot become an end in itself. All the same, as the fruit of centuries of experience, this method should not be undervalued. In its favor one could cite the experiences of countless Saints. This is not to say that the method cannot be improved. Such is the intent of the addition of the new series of *mysteria lucis* to the overall cycle of mysteries and of the few suggestions which I am proposing in this letter regarding the manner of recitation. These suggestions, while respecting the well-established structure of this prayer, are intended to help the faithful to understand it in the richness of its symbolism and in harmony with the demands of daily life. Other wise there is a risk that the Rosary would not only fail to produce the intended spiritual effects, but even that the beads, with which it is usually said, could come to be regarded as some kind of amulet or magic object, thereby radically distorting their meaning and function.[2]

These Bible studies enable the participants to progress from having a mental image of the Mysteries of Christ to having an in-depth understanding of the Biblical teachings regarding these mysteries. "Faith comes through hearing and what is heard is the word of Christ" (Romans 10:17). It is our fervent prayer that this understanding will lead to an intimate spiritual relationship with Jesus Christ. Pope John Paul II expressed this desire when he said:

> The cycles of meditation proposed by the Holy Rosary are by no means exhaustive, but they bring to mind what is essential and they awaken in the soul a thirst for knowledge

of Christ continually nourished by the pure source of the Gospel. Every individual event in the life of Christ, as narrated by the Evangelists, is resplendent with the Mystery that surpasses all understanding (cf. Eph 3:19): the Mystery of the Word made flesh, in whom "all the fullness of God dwells bodily" (Col 2:9). For this reason the *Catechism of the Catholic Church* places great emphasis on the mysteries of Christ, pointing out that "everything in the life of Jesus is a sign of his Mystery. The *"duc in altum"* of the Church in the third millennium will be determined by the ability of Christians to enter into the "perfect knowledge of God's mystery, of Christ in whom are hidden all the treasures of wisdom and knowledge" (Col 2:2-3). The letter to the Ephesians makes this heartfelt prayer for all the baptized: "May Christ dwell in your hearts through faith, so that you, being rooted and grounded in love, may have power... to know the love of Christ which surpasses knowledge, that you be filled with all the fullness of God" (Eph 3:17-19).[3]

It is our sincere hope that St. Paul's prayer may become a reality in the hearts of those who study and meditate on the Mysteries of Christ so that the fullness of Christ may dwell in their hearts and they will be filled with all the fullness of God. Glory be to the Father, and to the Son, and to the Holy Spirit; as it was in the beginning, is now, and ever shall be, world without end. Amen.

End Notes

[1]   John Paul II, *Apostolic Letter Rosarium Virginis Mariae of the Supreme Pontiff* http://www.vatican.va/holy_father/john_paul_ii/apost_letters/documents/hf_jp-ii_apl_20021016_rosarium-virginis-mariae_en.html

[2]   John Paul II, *Apostolic Letter,* 15.

[3]   John Paul II, *Apostolic Letter,* 13.

Made in the USA
Monee, IL
13 July 2024

61336784R00115